VOL. 65

COVERS ALL GRUMMAN & GENERAL MOTORS VERSIONS

F4F
Wildcat

in detail

Bert Kinzey

squadron/signal publications

COPYRIGHT © 2000 BY DETAIL & SCALE, INC.

This book is a product of Detail & Scale, Inc., which has sole responsibility for its content and layout, except that all contributors are responsible for the security clearance and copyright release of all materials submitted. Published by Squadron/Signal Publications, 1115 Crowley Drive, Carrollton, Texas 75011.

CONTRIBUTORS AND SOURCES:

Stan Piet	Stan Parker	National Archives
Lloyd Jones	Bob Bartolacci	National Museum of Naval Aviation, Pensacola, Florida
Larry Webster	Jim Galloway	Marine Corps Museum, Quantico, Virginia
Glen Phillips	Grumman History Center	Yanks Air Museum, Chino, California
Jason C. Bahr	U. S. Navy	Cavanaugh Flight Museum, Addison, Texas
Keith Liles	U. S. Marine Corps	National Air & Space Museum, Washington, D. C.

Detail & Scale, Inc. and the author express a sincere word of appreciation to Hill Goodspeed at the National Museum of Naval Aviation for his cooperation and assistance during the research for this publication. Thanks is also expressed to the museum's director, Captain Robert L. Rasmussen, USN (Ret.), and his staff who permitted the author to take numerous detailed photographs of four restored Wildcats that are on display at the museum.

A special thanks is also expressed to Mike Starn at the Marine Corps Museum at Quantico, Virginia, for his help in photographing the F4F-4 that is on display there. Additional thanks goes to the Yanks Air Museum at Chino, California, the National Air & Space Museum in Washington, D. C., and the Cavanaugh Flight Museum in Addison, Texas.

Many photographs in this publication are credited to their contributors. Photographs with no credit indicated were taken by the author.

ISBN 1-888974-18-4

Above, front cover photo: An F4F-4 displays the Blue-Gray over Light Gray camouflage scheme and the markings used in early 1942 as it flies over Long Island near the Grumman plant at Bethpage, New York.
(National Archives)

Right: An overall view from the right side shows the major details on the instrument panel in an FM-2. For additional color photographs of the cockpit in this Wildcat, see pages 44 and 45.

INTRODUCTION

Armorers work above and below the wings to reload the six guns in an F4F-4 Wildcat. Note the three ammunition boxes on the ground below each wing. The boxes were loaded up through the bottom of the wings, then the ends of the ammunition belts would be positioned into the machine guns. The small bomb racks are also visible in place under each wing. (National Archives)

In 1988, Detail & Scale produced a book on the Grumman Wildcat. At that time, there were only two accurately restored Wildcats in existence. Other examples were mostly FM-2s that were in the hands of private owners, and these usually had modern radios and other equipment installed. As a result, that book relied almost exclusively on black and white general and detailed photographs obtained from Grumman's excellent history center in Bethpage, New York. It is unfortunate to note that since that book was written, Grumman has merged with Northrop, and the outstanding history center is no longer a funded operation of the aerospace company. It was arguably the best of its kind in the world, and it is a shame to see it discontinued.

The Wildcat is one of the World War II aircraft for which very little original color photography is available. Therefore, many of the color photos in that book were of the privately owned aircraft, and these did not accurately represent color schemes for the FM-2.

In the years since that book was released, several Wildcats have been restored accurately to their original configurations. These include an F4F-3, F4F-3A, and two FM-2s at the National Museum of Naval Aviation in Pensacola, Florida. One of these FM-2s has now been traded to another owner, but it was photographed extensively by the author before the trade was made. The Marine Corps Museum at Quantico, Virginia, has the only restored F4F-4 on display anywhere in the world, and the National Air & Space Museum has an excellent FM-1 in its collection.

For this new book on the Wildcat, trips were made to photograph all of these aircraft in detail. Additionally, the FM-2 at the Yanks Air Museum in Chino, California, was photographed as was the one at the Cavanaugh Flight Museum in Addison, Texas. Dozens of these detailed photographs appear in this publication, and many are included in the color section. Cockpits in the F4F-3, F4F-4, and FM-2 are illustrated in color as are both the Pratt & Whitney R-1830 and Wright R-1820 powerplants.

In some cases, Grumman photos are used again, because they are the best or only pictures available to show design features and details of certain aircraft. For the most part, these are limited to experimental versions or aircraft that existed for only a short period of time. Otherwise, the detailed photographs are new and were taken specifically for this publication. Some historical photographs are used again as well, but many new ones have also been included from the archives of the National Museum of Naval Aviation.

New 1/72nd scale drawings have been completed for this book by Lloyd S. Jones, and they show the changes made to the aircraft throughout its development. Three pages of color profiles have also been added to illustrate the development of paint schemes and markings used on the Wildcat.

In the twelve years that have passed since our first book was released, new and better kits of the Wildcat have been released in 1/72nd and 1/48th scales, and these are covered in our usual Modelers Summary at the end of the book.

With dozens of new photographs, twice as much color including color profiles, new 1/72nd scale drawings, and a new text and captions, this book presents a far more complete and detailed look at the Wildcat than was possible in our previous book twelve years ago.

DEVELOPMENTAL HISTORY
XF4F-1 1/72nd SCALE DRAWING

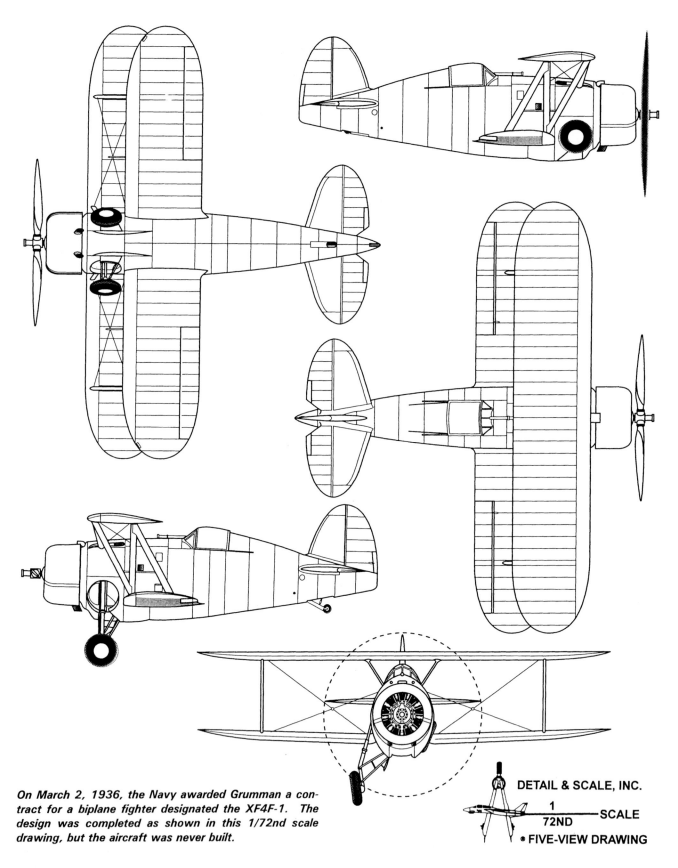

On March 2, 1936, the Navy awarded Grumman a contract for a biplane fighter designated the XF4F-1. The
design was completed as shown in this 1/72nd scale
drawing, but the aircraft was never built.

DETAIL & SCALE, INC.

$$\frac{1}{72ND}$$ SCALE

● FIVE-VIEW DRAWING

DETAIL & SCALE, 1/72nd SCALE COPYRIGHT © DRAWINGS BY LLOYD S. JONES

On September 2, 1937, Robert L. Hall piloted the XF4F-2 on its initial flight from Grumman's facility at Bethpage, New York. (Grumman)

In any technology, there are periods of rapid advancement where old ways of doing things are quickly replaced with completely new and different methods and procedures. The development of aviation has seen more than its share of such periods, and the first of these happened during the mid-1930s. Up until that time, most aircraft had been biplane designs, but the advantages of the all-metal monoplane were obvious, at least on paper. When new advancements are so radical, it is only natural to hold on to that which is established as being reliable until it is certain that the new technology is also dependable. It was this cautious approach that, on November 15, 1935, prompted the Navy to approve both the design of the XF4F-1 along with a monoplane proposed by Brewster that would eventually become the F2A Buffalo. Fearing that Brewster's monoplane may have developmental and operational problems, the Navy considered the XF4F-1 to be an insurance policy, since it was a proven and conservative biplane design.

On March 2, 1936, the Navy awarded Grumman a contract for construction of the XF4F-1, and this was followed by a contract to Brewster for a prototype of the XF2A on June 22. Meanwhile, the performance figures for the XF4F-1 were calculated to be only marginally better than Grumman's existing F3F biplane that was already in service. For example, top speed was projected to increase by only ten miles per hour. This caused the Navy to rethink its policy, and it was realized that an-

other biplane was not necessary if it wasn't going to be much better than what was already in service. It therefore seemed wiser to have Grumman also develop a new monoplane design as a competitor to the Brewster XF2A, because there was a higher probability of success with two monoplanes than one. As a result, the Navy canceled the XF4F-1, and on July 10, 1936, they approved a change to the XF4F-2 monoplane. A formal contract for a single XF4F-2 prototype followed on July 28.

Although the contract for the XF4F-2 was awarded just over a month after the one to Brewster, Grumman completed its prototype first, and on September 2, 1937, Robert L. Hall took the aircraft up for its maiden flight. The XF2A-1 did not fly until December of that year.

Initial tests with the XF4F-2 were conducted at Grumman for four months, then the aircraft was flown to NAS Anacostia, Maryland, for further trials by the Navy. In March 1938, competitive evaluations were begun with the XF4F-2, the XF2A-1, and Seversky's XNF-1, the latter of which was in the same family as the Army's P-35. The competition proved that the XF4F-2 was the fastest of the three aircraft, but the top speed of 290 miles per hour still fell short of the 300 miles per hour goal. The Pratt & Whitney R-1830-66 powerplant experienced bearing failures, and these, along with some stability problems, resulted in the selection of the XF2A as the winner of the competition. The production F2A would go on to be the Navy's first operational monoplane fighter,

The first production version of the Wildcat was the F4F-3. A few, like this one assigned to VF-4, were delivered in the Navy's colorful pre-war paint schemes. This photo was taken at Bethpage in December 1940. Note that the diagonal white stripes were applied to the underside of the wings as well as the top on this particular Wildcat.

(NMNA)

Although the United States was not yet a combatant in World War II, a Navy directive, dated December 30, 1940, ordered that the colorful paint schemes be replaced with a low-visibility Light Gray scheme. This F4F-3 was assigned to VF-71 and based at NAS Norfolk, Virginia, in the spring of 1941. A color profile of this aircraft appears on page 33.

(NMNA)

but its service life was plagued with difficulties, and its performance was always considered substandard.

On April 11, the aircraft experienced a forced landing in a field, but the aircraft was salvageable. Although it did not win the competition, the Navy had Grumman continue to work on the bugs that troubled the XF4F-2 just in case things did not go well for the F2A Buffalo, and in October 1938, the Navy issued a contract for an improved version of the design. Grumman went to work on the damaged XF4F-2, changing the wing and tail surfaces to correct the stability problems, and installing an improved XR-1830-76 version of Pratt & Whitney's radial engine with a two-stage, two-speed supercharger. This solved the problem with the bearing failures while significantly improving performance at the same time. BuNo. 0383 was reborn as the XF4F-3. In this new configuration, the XF4F-3 made its first flight on February 12, 1939. During subsequent flight tests, a top speed of over 333 miles per hour was attained.

After testing by both Grumman and the Navy, the aircraft again entered the plant at Bethpage for more modifications to the design. The tail section was totally reworked to the design that would remain standard for all Wildcats to come except for the XF4F-8 and FM-2. In its second configuration, the basic appearance of the Wildcat was established. Problems with engine overheating continued, and spinners of various sizes and shapes were tried to solve this problem. But these were not significant, and the Wildcat was ready to enter production.

The F4F-3 was the first production variant for the Navy, and an initial order of fifty-four aircraft was placed on August 8, 1939. Two months later, France ordered one hundred export versions to serve on the two aircraft carriers it then had under construction. The French aircraft had several differences from the F4F-3, and most notable of these was a change to the Wright R-1820 powerplant.

The first production F4F-3 flew in February 1940, and this was followed in May by the initial flight of a French aircraft. But shortly thereafter, France was overrun by Germany, and the French order was taken over by the British who named the aircraft the Martlet. Those from the French order became Martlet Is, and a total of 1,102 Martlets would be supplied to the Royal Navy in six different versions before the end of the war. On December 25, 1940, a Martlet I shot down a German Ju-88 bomber near Scapa Flow, off Scotland, thus scoring the first kill by an aircraft of the F4F family.

Deliveries to U. S. Navy squadrons began in December 1940, with VF-4 from USS RANGER (CV-4) and VF-7 from USS WASP (CV-7) being the first to receive the new fighter. These two squadrons were redesignated VF-41 and VF-72 respectively in March 1941.

Greece also ordered a version of the new fighter which was identical to the F4F-3 except that it had the R-1830-90 powerplant instead of the R-1830-76 used in the F4F-3. The Navy designated these aircraft F4F-3As, but before they could be delivered to Greece, that country was invaded by Axis forces. As a result, thirty went to the Royal Navy as Martlet IIIs and the remainder were assigned to the U. S. Navy as F4F-3As. The first of these entered service with VF-6 in May 1941. Deliveries continued, and by the end of 1941, 181 F4F-3s and F4F-3As were in service with the U. S. Navy and Marines.

The first taste of combat by American Wildcats was decidedly a bitter one as nine out of eleven of VMF-211's F4F-3s were destroyed on the ground when the Japanese attacked Pearl Harbor on December 7, 1941. The following day, Japan attacked Wake Island, and destroyed seven of twelve Wildcats which had been flown there only four days earlier. Four operational Wildcats were part of the Marines' valiant defense of the island, but the superior Japanese forces prevailed and eventually overran the island on December 23.

By the end of the year, production of the F4F-4 had begun. This new version featured folding wings for carrier operations, and armament was increased to six .50-caliber machine guns in the wings instead of only four.

In January 1942, the Eastern Aircraft Division of General Motors changed from the production of automobiles to aircraft. It would eventually take over production of the Grumman's Wildcat fighter and Avenger torpedo bomber. By war's end, Eastern would build more of each type than Grumman would. This permitted Grumman to concentrate its efforts on the F6F Hellcat throughout most of the war. Later, it would also build the F7F Tigercat and F8F Bearcat.

The Wildcat's first action with the U. S. Navy began in February 1942 when U. S. carriers began a series of strikes against Japanese held islands in the Pacific. On February 20, Lt. Edward "Butch" O'Hare became the Navy's first ace by shooting down five Japanese bombers that were attacking the carrier USS LEXINGTON, CV-2. These hit and run raids continued for several months, then, in the first week of May, the Battle of the Coral Sea became the first major action between forces of the United States and Japan. It was also the first naval battle fought between carriers and the first where ships of the opposing forces never came within sight of each other.

The following month, the Battle of Midway dealt the Imperial Japanese Navy a crippling blow by sinking four of its carriers. This stopped the Japanese advance across the Pacific, and again the Wildcats were there to play a significant role. A total of eighty-one F4F-4s were aboard the carriers ENTERPRISE, YORKTOWN, and HORNET. Seven Marine F4F-3s were also based on Midway Island. In spite of the Wildcat's inferior performance to the vaunted Japanese Zero, they shot down three Japanese aircraft to each Wildcat that was lost.

F4F-4s of VF-8 prepare to launch from USS HORNET, CV-8, on June 4, 1942, during the pivotal Battle of Midway. (NMNA)

Wildcats also operated from land bases with Marine squadrons. Here F4F-4s of VMF-121 are ready to launch from Henderson Field on Guadalcanal. **(NMNA)**

During the second half of 1942, Marine Wildcats were assigned to land bases in the Southwest Pacific. On August 20, nineteen Marine Wildcats became the first U. S. fighters to arrive on Guadalcanal, and over the next few months, they scored remarkable victories over the Japanese. Among the pilots was Joe Foss, who became the Marine Corps' leading ace with twenty-six victories, all of which were scored in Wildcats. In all, thirty-four Marines and twenty-seven Navy pilots became aces flying Wildcats. For the most part, these aerial victories were scored in the early years, because the Wildcats were being replaced by F6F Hellcats and F4U Corsairs in front line squadrons by the middle of 1943. But Wildcats would continue to be used in important support roles for the remainder of the war.

In the Atlantic, Wildcats and British Martlets took part in Operation Torch, the invasion of North Africa. But the primary role played by Wildcats and Martlets in the Atlantic was flown from the small escort carriers. Composite air groups, consisting of Wildcats and Avengers, flew from the CVEs to provide air cover above the convoys moving between the United States and England.

These escort carriers and their aircraft played a critical role in protecting the convoys from German U-boats. Wildcats, including F4F-4s, FM-1s and FM-2s, also operated from escort carriers until the end of the war in the Pacific. Primary among their roles was that of providing close air support to American ground forces battling the Japanese on the islands and atolls of the Pacific.

It was the final version of the Wildcat which was delivered in the greatest numbers. The FM-2, produced by Eastern Aircraft, was lighter than the earlier versions, and it had a more powerful Wright R-1820-56 engine. Its performance was better than the Pratt & Whitney powered versions, and it was ideally suited for operations from the smaller escort carriers.

The Wildcat has often been criticized for its lack of performance when compared to the Japanese Zero, most German fighters, and other Allied fighters that appeared later in the war. But its achievements in combat were outstanding, and its contributions to final victory cannot be overstated. The author has had the privilege to talk to many Wildcat pilots from World War II including several aces. Among these are Joe Foss and the late Marion Carl. Given a choice, every one of them stated that they would prefer to go into combat in the Wildcat over any Japanese fighter they faced. Many owe their lives to the superior firepower and rugged design of Grumman's barrel shaped fighter. Those strengths proved to be far more important than the Zero's maneuverability, speed, and rate of climb. As Scott McCusky, who scored 6 1/3 victories in Wildcats and seven in Hellcats, explained, "Unless you tried to fight a Japanese fighter on his terms or did something stupid, you were not at a real disadvantage in the Wildcat. He could climb away from you, but you could dive away from him. In the F4F, we were not going to score a kill in every fight, but we never felt that we were at a disadvantage where we were going to lose."

The Wildcat was the only Navy fighter to serve throughout the entire war from the attack on Pearl Harbor until VJ Day. That is a tribute not only to its design but to the importance of the role it played in the eventual defeat of Axis forces in both the Atlantic and the Pacific.

This FM-2 was assigned to VC-84 aboard USS MAKIN ISLAND, CVE-93, in late 1944 and early 1945. It is armed with six five-inch rockets which were often used to support American ground forces battling the Japanese on the islands of the Pacific. **(NMNA)**

Another FM-2 from VC-84 is respotted on the flight deck of USS MAKIN ISLAND. FM-2s served in composite squadrons with TBM Avengers aboard escort carriers, and both types of aircraft were Grumman designs built by General Motors' Eastern Aircraft Division. **(NMNA)**

WILDCAT VARIANTS
XF4F-2

Only one XF4F-2, BuNo. 0383, was built, and it was quite different from the production Wildcats that followed. Note the machine gun mounted in the cowling, the large antenna mast on the forward fuselage, and the telescopic sight in the windscreen. The original short cowling is also evident in this side view. (Grumman)

After the contract for the XF4F-1 biplane was canceled on July 10, 1936, it was quickly replaced with contract number 46973 for the XF4F-2 monoplane on July 28. Only one prototype was to be built, and the Navy assigned it BuNo. 0383. Grumman's employees worked quickly, knowing that Brewster had a head start with their XF2A. As a result of their efforts, the XF4F-2 was the first to fly when Robert L. Hall took the aircraft up for its initial flight on September 2, 1937. The XF2A did not fly until December of that year.

As completed, the XF4F-2 was an all metal mono-plane of mid-wing design. The ailerons, elevators, and rudder were metal framework covered with fabric. External counterbalances were located on top of the elevators. Pneumatically operated split flaps spanned the entire trailing edge of the wings between the fuselage and the ailerons. A Pratt & Whitney R-1830-66, having fourteen cylinders in two rows, was chosen as the powerplant, and it was augmented with a single speed supercharger. This engine produced 1,050 horsepower for takeoff, and at 12,000 feet, 900 horsepower was available. Carburetor air was taken in through a scoop on top of the forward fuselage.

The XF4F-2 had rounded tips on the wings and all tail surfaces, and there were large external counterbalances on the tops of the elevators. Two windows were located on each side of the lower fuselage beneath the wings. (Grumman)

During its flight testing, the XF4F-2's propeller was fitted with spinners of various shapes and sizes. These were part of an effort to solve overheating problems with the engine. Compare this later photograph to the two earlier ones on the previous page, and notice that the cowling is longer and has a different shape. *(Grumman)*

Problems with engine overheating were experienced early in the flight testing, so the cowling was redesigned and two cooling flaps were added. Spinners of various shapes and sizes were also tied to help alleviate the overheating problems, but they were never completely solved until near the end of the F4F-3 production run. Of a more critical nature, the R-1830-66 experienced bearing failures that Pratt & Whitney worked diligently to correct.

Armament consisted of two .30-caliber machine guns mounted in the cowling, and provisions were made for two .50-caliber guns in the wings. Two hundred rounds of ammunition was supplied for each weapon, and a telescopic sight was mounted through the windscreen. A rack could be attached under each wing to carry bombs in the 100-pound class.

After testing by Grumman, the XF4F-2 was delivered to the Navy on December 23, 1937. The first problem occurred on February 16, 1938, when an in-flight fire was experienced, but the aircraft landed successfully back at Bethpage with minimal damage. Two days later, tests continued at NAS Dahlgren, and by March 1, it was ready to be flown in competition against the Brewster XF2A and Seversky's XNF-1. The following month, the XF4F-2 was flown to Philadelphia for carrier evaluations including catapult launches and arrested recoveries. Shortly thereafter, a forced landing on April 11 caused the aircraft to flip over on its back, and it received considerable damage. Nevertheless, it was salvageable, so it was shipped back to Grumman's factory on Long Island.

In June 1938, the Navy officially selected Brewster's XF2A as the winner of the competition held the previous March, and the F2A Buffalo thus became the Navy's first

monoplane fighter. But the wrecked XF4F-2 would be redesigned and rebuilt to fly again as the XF4F-3.

DATA

Version	XF4F-2
Grumman Model Number	G-18
Number Built	1
Armament	4 X .50-caliber machine guns
Powerplant	Pratt & Whitney R-1830-66
Horsepower	1,000
Maximum Speed	288 mph at 10,000 feet
Landing Speed	72 mph
Rate of Climb	2,659 feet-per-minute
Ceiling	30,000 feet
Maximum Range	740 miles
Wingspan	34 feet
Length	26 feet, 5 inches
Height	11 feet, 10.5 inches
Empty Weight	3,980 pounds
Gross Weight	5,231 pounds
Maximum Internal Fuel	130 gallons
External Fuel	None

From the beginning, Grumman included the capability for the Wildcat to carry a small bomb of the 100-pound class under each wing. The carburetor scoop on top of the forward fuselage is visible in this view. *(Grumman)*

XF4F-2 DETAILS

The instrument panel in the XF4F-2 was similar to the ones that would follow in early production aircraft.
(Grumman)

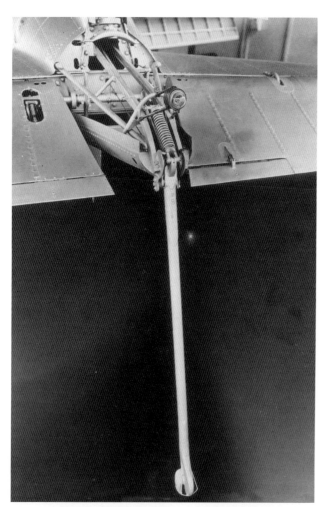

Details of the tail hook are revealed in this factory photograph. The tail cone has been removed to provide a look at the structure to which the hook was attached and the slides on which it moved. A small light is mounted on the structure above the hook. *(Grumman)*

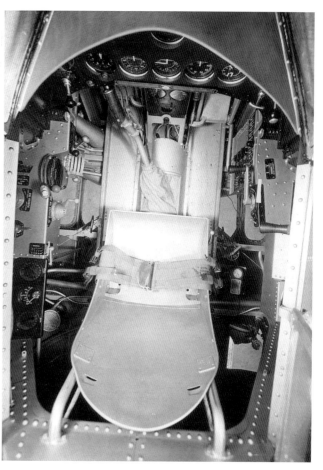

There was no floor in the cockpit so that the pilot could look down through the four windows in the lower fuselage. *(Grumman)*

Panels on the right side of the forward fuselage have been opened or removed to reveal details of the machine gun. Note the long blast tube on the muzzle of the weapon. Two hundred rounds of ammunition were carried for each cowl gun. *(Grumman)*

XF4F-2 1/72nd SCALE DRAWINGS (ORIGINAL CONFIGURATION)

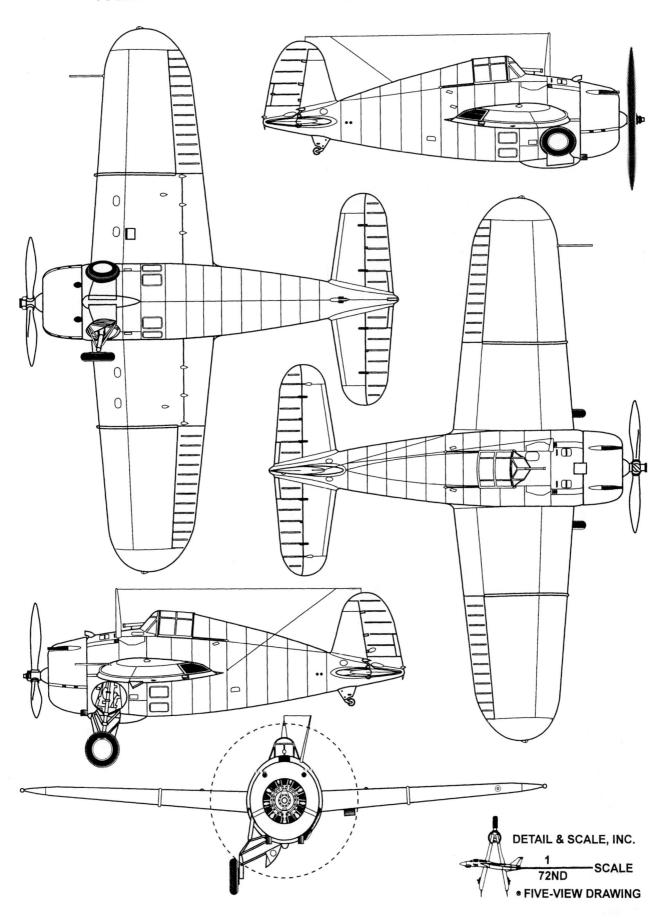

DETAIL & SCALE, INC.

$\dfrac{1}{72ND}$ SCALE

● FIVE-VIEW DRAWING

DETAIL & SCALE, 1/72nd SCALE COPYRIGHT © DRAWINGS BY LLOYD S. JONES

XF4F-3

After the XF4F-2 was damaged in a crash landing, it was rebuilt to the first of two XF4F-3 configurations. Most noticeable were the blunt tips on the wing and tail surfaces instead of the rounded ones used on the XF4F-2. Note that the BuNo. 0383 was retained. **(Grumman)**

Although the XF4F-2 lost out to Brewster's XF2A in the competition during March 1938, it was the fastest of the three aircraft in that evaluation, and its further development offered insurance in the event the F2A did not meet the expectations the Navy held for it. In October

An underside view provides a good look at the blunt tips on the wings and horizontal tail. **(Grumman)**

1938, Grumman received a contract for development of the XF4F-3. The damaged XF4F-2, BuNo 0383, would be used again as the prototype.

Grumman increased the wingspan to thirty-eight feet, and the wings, horizontal tail surfaces, and the vertical tail were all redesigned. The rounded tips, used on the XF4F-2, were replaced with blunt tips, and these helped solve the stability problems. Pratt & Whitney delivered the XR-1830-76, and this eliminated the problems with bearing failures. The intake scoop for carburetor air was moved from the top of the forward fuselage to the top of the cowl ring. Additionally, the new engine had a two-stage, two-speed supercharger which offered better performance at higher altitudes. An intercooler was placed between the two stages, and cooling air was brought in by two scoops located inside the cowling. Although this was a gamble on Grumman's part, it was to prove effective. The new powerplant could deliver 1,200 horsepower for takeoff and 1,000 horsepower at 19,000 feet. This was a considerable increase over that provided by the R-1830-66 used in the XF4F-2.

In its new configuration, the XF4F-3 made its first flight on February 12, 1939, and again, Robert L. Hall was at the controls. The following month it was flown to NAS Anacostia, Maryland, for testing by the Navy. These tests demonstrated that the stability problems had been corrected to a degree, but there was still work to do. The dihedral of the wing was increased, and the span of the ailerons was reduced. Further evaluations in NACA's wind tunnels at Langley, Virginia, revealed a need to redesign the entire tail section once again, so the aircraft was returned to Grumman. The horizontal tail was moved from its location on the fuselage to a position low on the vertical stabilizer. The entire vertical tail was redesigned and faired into the spine of the fuselage. The large antenna mast on the fuselage was replaced by a smaller mast mounted at an angle on the spine of the aircraft. Test flights in the final configuration resulted in a top speed of 333 miles per hour.

Like the XF4F-2, armament in the XF4F-3 consisted of machine guns mounted in the cowling and wings.

In its final configuration, the vertical tail of the XF4F-3 was redesigned, and the horizontal tail was moved up from the fuselage to a low position on the vertical stabilizer. Except for the taller vertical tail used on the FM-2, this design would remain unchanged on all production Wildcats. Note that there is no spinner on the propeller hub, and the large antenna mast on the forward fuselage has been deleted in favor of a smaller mast on the spine of the aircraft behind the cockpit. *(Grumman)*

Also like the XF4F-2, the XF4F-3 experienced persistent problems with engine overheating. A variety of spinners continued to be evaluated, and although the problems were under control, they were not yet fully solved.

Throughout the remainder of 1939 and 1940, the XF4F-3 continued to be used for various tests and evaluations. In November 1940, the XF4F-3 flew carrier qualifications aboard USS RANGER, CV-4, and USS WASP, CV-7, the Navy's smallest fleet carriers. Squadrons from these two carriers were scheduled to be the first to transition to the F4F-3.

On December 17, with a total of 345.4 hours of flying time, the XF4F-3 crashed at NAS Norfolk killing LTJG. W. C. Johnson who mistakenly turned off the fuel selector valve instead of actuating the flap selector. Although the destruction of the aircraft and loss of the pilot was unfortunate, production of the F4F-3 was well underway, and aircraft of the French order were being delivered to the Royal Navy. Initial deliveries to the first Navy squadrons were begun that same month.

In retrospect, the Navy's decision to continue the development of the XF4F-2 and the XF4F-3 proved to be one of the most important made in the history of naval aviation. Brewster's F2A Buffalo turned out to be en-tirely inadequate for combat in World War II, and had the F4F Wildcat not been available, the Navy and Marines would have had to fight the first eighteen months of the war with the Buffalo as their primary fighter. Although the Wildcat may have not had the performance offered by later designs, it proved more than adequate to hold the line until the Hellcats and Corsairs became available in large numbers.

DATA

Version	XF4F-3
Grumman Model Number	G-36
Number Built	1*
Armament	2 X .30-caliber machine guns & 2 X .50-caliber machine guns in the wings
Powerplant	Pratt & Whitney XR 1830-76
Horsepower	1,200
Maximum Speed	335 mph at 21,300
Cruising Speed	198 mph
Initial Rate of Climb	2,500 feet-per-minute
Ceiling	33,500 feet
Maximum Range	1,300 miles
Combat Range	890 miles
Wingspan	38 feet
Length	28 feet
Height	11 feet, 9 inches
Empty Weight	4,794 pounds
Gross Weight	6,305 pounds
Maximum Internal Fuel	161 gallons
External Fuel	None

* This was the same airframe, BuNo. 0383, used for the XF4F-2 as rebuilt after the aircraft crash landed.

Details of the instrument panel in the XF4F-3 are revealed in this low view beneath the top shield. *(Grumman)*

A telescopic sight was mounted to the shield above the instrument panel, and it extended through the forward glass of the windscreen. An iron ring and bead sight was attached to the telescopic sight. *(NMNA)*

XF4F-3 1/72nd SCALE DRAWINGS

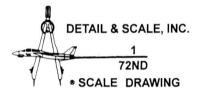

DETAIL & SCALE, INC.

$\dfrac{1}{72\text{ND}}$

® SCALE DRAWING

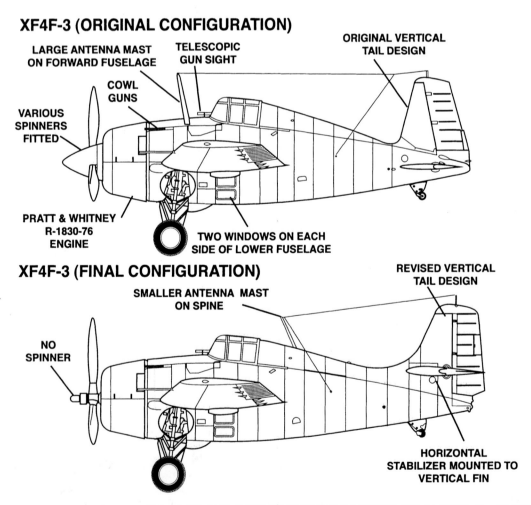

XF4F-3 (ORIGINAL CONFIGURATION)

LARGE ANTENNA MAST ON FORWARD FUSELAGE

TELESCOPIC GUN SIGHT

ORIGINAL VERTICAL TAIL DESIGN

COWL GUNS

VARIOUS SPINNERS FITTED

PRATT & WHITNEY R-1830-76 ENGINE

TWO WINDOWS ON EACH SIDE OF LOWER FUSELAGE

XF4F-3 (FINAL CONFIGURATION)

REVISED VERTICAL TAIL DESIGN

SMALLER ANTENNA MAST ON SPINE

NO SPINNER

HORIZONTAL STABILIZER MOUNTED TO VERTICAL FIN

DETAIL & SCALE, 1/72nd SCALE COPYRIGHT © DRAWING BY LLOYD S. JONES

F4F-3 & F4F-3A

BuNo. 1844 was the first production F4F-3. The first two F4F-3s retained the cowl guns found on the XF4F-2 and XF4F-3, but beginning with the third F4F-3, these were deleted in favor of four .50-caliber machine guns in the wings. This Wildcat had the telescopic gun sight mounted through the windshield. (Grumman)

The second F4F-3, BuNo. 1845, makes a test flight over Long Island. As production of the F4F-3 began, spinners were still being tested in an attempt to provide adequate cooling air to the engine. Also note the rounded windscreen without the telescopic sight or the plate of armored glass. (Grumman)

The initial production version of the Wildcat was the F4F-3, and the first two of these were designated for service tests. BuNo. 1844 made its maiden flight in February 1940, and it was followed by BuNo. 1845 in July. Both of these aircraft had the same armament as the XF4F-3 to include the two machine guns in the cowling. Subsequent production F4F-3s had four .50-caliber machine guns in the wings. Unfortunately, BuNo. 1844 was lost in a crash in March 1941. BuNo. 1845 was used for drop tests with 100-pound bombs, then later it conducted carrier qualifications. These revealed a need for a stronger landing gear, and the tail gear was slightly enlarged as it was strengthened. The third and fourth F4F-3s, BuNos. 1846 and 1847, were used for evaluation with the Wright R-1820 engine, and these were redesignated XF4F-5s. The evaluation with the R-1820 was undertaken, because it was the powerplant that was to be installed in the aircraft ordered by the French.

The R-1830-76 was installed in the first batch of F4F-3, but problems with overheating continued, and as a result, the single cooling flap on each side of the cowling was eventually replaced with four on each side on the later production blocks. The engine itself was changed to the R-1830-86 in the second production batch. These could be identified by the two magnetos mounted on top of the crankcase. Throughout production, the cowling went through several design changes, and these are

The fifth F4F-3, BuNo. 1848, was assigned to the executive officer of VF-4, and it is shown here as it appeared at Bethpage in December 1940. The tail is green, indicating assignment to USS RANGER, CV-4, and the top of the cowling is red. The squadron crest is red and dark blue. VF-4 was redesignated VF-41 in March 1941, and this change appears to be anticipated, because a space where the 1 will be added has been left available in the fuselage code. (NMNA)

F4F-3, BuNo. 1880, was assigned to VF-72 aboard USS WASP, CV-7. Note the different location of the fuselage insignia on the cowling as compared to the one on the Wildcat in the photograph at left. This fuselage insignia was a neutrality marking. Aircraft assigned to WASP during this time frame had gloss black tail surfaces. The cowl ring and fuselage band are yellow outlined in black. A color profile of this aircraft appears on page 33. (Grumman)

The F4F-3A was the same as the F4F-3 except that it was powered by a Pratt & Whitney R-1830-90 engine instead of the R-1830-76. This is the first F4F-3A, BuNo. 3905, shortly after completion at the Grumman plant. This was the first aircraft to have the small tear-drop shaped fairing between the cowling and the landing gear. Also note that the scoop for carburetor air is present on the top of the cowl ring, however the F4F-3As did not have the intakes for intercooler air inside the cowling. *(Grumman)*

The two guns in each wing are visible on this F4F-3 from VF-2 as it prepares to launch from USS ENTERPRISE, CV-6, on May 12, 1942. *(National Archives)*

illustrated on page 17.

The first F4F-3s that were delivered to Navy squadrons VF-4 and VF-7 looked very much like the final configuration of the XF4F-3, except for the deletion of the cowl guns. Another noticeable change was that there was only one window on each side of the lower fuselage rather than two.

After VF-4 and VF-7 received their aircraft, deliveries continued to VF-42. The first Marine units to receive the F4F-3 were VMF-222, VMF-223, and VMF-214, with VMF-221, VMF-211, and VMF-121 following a few months later. VF-3 and VF-5 were the last units to receive the F4F-3 in September 1941. No F4F-3s were produced in 1942, but Grumman reopened the F4F-3 production line in 1943. One hundred additional F4F-3s, BuNos. 12230 through 12329, were delivered during the first five months of that year, and these aircraft were used for stateside training purposes only. A total of 285 F4F-3s were delivered, and of these, BuNos. 2512, 2517, 2526, 2530, 2537, 3985, and 3997 were delivered with camera installations as F4F-3Ps.

One aircraft was fitted with an R-1830-90 engine that had only a single-stage, two-speed supercharger. This version of the R-1830 did not have the intercooler, because it only had one stage. Therefore the two scoops for intercooler air were not present inside the cowling. This evaluation with the R-1830-90 was conducted in case problems developed with the more complex two-stage, two-speed versions of the engine. The prototype was originally designated the XF4F-6, but this was soon changed to XF4F-3A. Ninety-five production F4F-3As followed, all of which were equipped with the R-1830-90.

The first thirty F4F-3As were intended for delivery to Greece, but these were diverted to the Royal Navy as Martlet IIIs when Greece was invaded by the Axis. The remaining sixty-five were delivered to the U. S. Navy and Marines beginning with VMF-111 in April 1941 and VF-6 in May 1941. VMF-212, VF-5, VF-2, and VF-3 were the other units to receive the F4F-3A.

DATA

Version	F4F-3 & F4F-3A
Grumman Model Number	G-36
Number Built:	
F4F-3	285
F4F-3A	95
Armament	4 X .50-caliber machine guns*
Powerplant:	
F4F-3	Pratt & Whitney R-1830-76 or -86
F4F-3A	Pratt & Whitney R-1830-90
Horsepower	1,200
Maximum Speed:	
F4F-3	330 mph at 22,000 feet
F4F-3A	312 mph at 16,000 feet
Cruising Speed:	
F4F-3	198 mph
F4F-3A	156 mph
Initial Rate of Climb:	
F4F-3	2,050 feet-per-minute
F4F-3A	2,430 feet-per-minute
Ceiling:	
F4F-3	32,600 feet
F4F-3A	34,300 feet
Maximum Range:	
F4F-3	1,800 miles
F4F-3A	1,585 miles
Combat Range:	
F4F-3	845 miles
F4F-3A	825 miles
Wingspan	38 feet
Length	28 feet, 10.5 inches
Height	11 feet, 9 inches
Empty Weight:	
F4F-3	5,293 pounds
F4F-3A	5,216 pounds
Gross Weight:	
F4F-3	7,467 pounds
F4F-3A	6,876 pounds
Maximum Take-off Weight:	
F4F-3	8,152 pounds
F4F-3A	8,026 pounds
Maximum Internal Fuel	147 gallons
External Fuel	2 X 58-gallon tanks

* The first two F4F-3s had the same armament as the XF4F-3.

F4F-3 COWLING DIFFERENCES

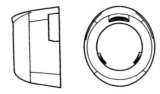

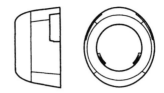

The cowling of the F4F-3 went through several design changes. The first configuration included a scoop for the carburetor at the top of the cowl ring. Two lower scoops inside the cowling provided air to the intercooler. A single cooling flap was located on each side of the cowling. This arrangement was used on the first F4F-3s including BuNos. 1848 through 1896 and 2512 through 2538. These Wildcats had the R-1830-76 engine.

BuNos. 3856 through 3874 were fitted with the R-1830-86 engine. These Wildcats did not have the scoop in the top of the cowl ring, but they did have the single cooling flap and the two intakes for intercooler air.

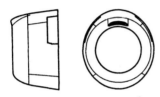

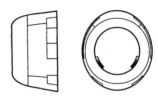

F4F-3As had R-1830-90 engines. These aircraft, BuNos. 3905 through 3969, had the intake for the carburetor air in the top of the cowl ring, but they did not have the two scoops inside the cowling for the intercooler air.

The final one hundred F4F-3s, BuNos. 12230 through 12329, did not have the carburetor scoop in the top of the cowl ring, but they did have the two scoops for the intercooler. To improve cooling of the engine, the single flap on each side was replaced with four smaller flaps. Three were grouped together while the bottom flap was mounted apart from the other three and was lower on the trailing edge of the cowling.

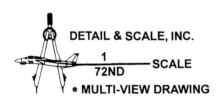

DETAIL & SCALE, INC.

$\frac{1}{72ND}$ SCALE

● MULTI-VIEW DRAWING

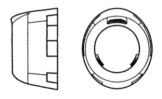

Photographs provide evidence that a few F4F-3s in the final production batch of one hundred had the carburetor scoop, intercooler scoops, and the four cooling flaps on each side, but this configuration actually became standard on the F4F-4.

F4F-3 1/72nd SCALE DRAWINGS

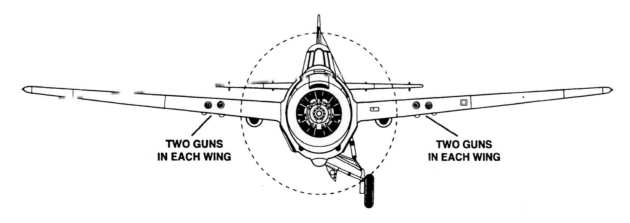

TWO GUNS IN EACH WING

TWO GUNS IN EACH WING

DETAIL & SCALE, 1/72nd SCALE COPYRIGHT © DRAWINGS BY LLOYD S. JONES

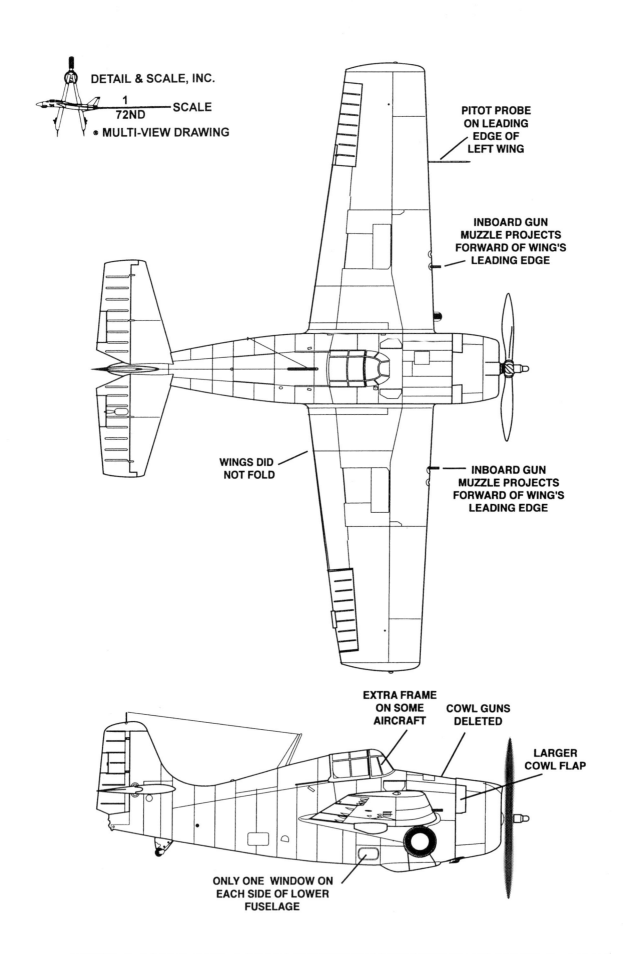

DETAIL & SCALE, INC.

$\frac{1}{72ND}$ —— SCALE

® MULTI-VIEW DRAWING

PITOT PROBE
ON LEADING
EDGE OF
LEFT WING

INBOARD GUN
MUZZLE PROJECTS
FORWARD OF WING'S
LEADING EDGE

INBOARD GUN
MUZZLE PROJECTS
FORWARD OF WING'S
LEADING EDGE

WINGS DID
NOT FOLD

EXTRA FRAME
ON SOME
AIRCRAFT

COWL GUNS
DELETED

LARGER
COWL FLAP

ONLY ONE WINDOW ON
EACH SIDE OF LOWER
FUSELAGE

DETAIL & SCALE, 1/72nd SCALE COPYRIGHT © DRAWINGS BY LLOYD S. JONES

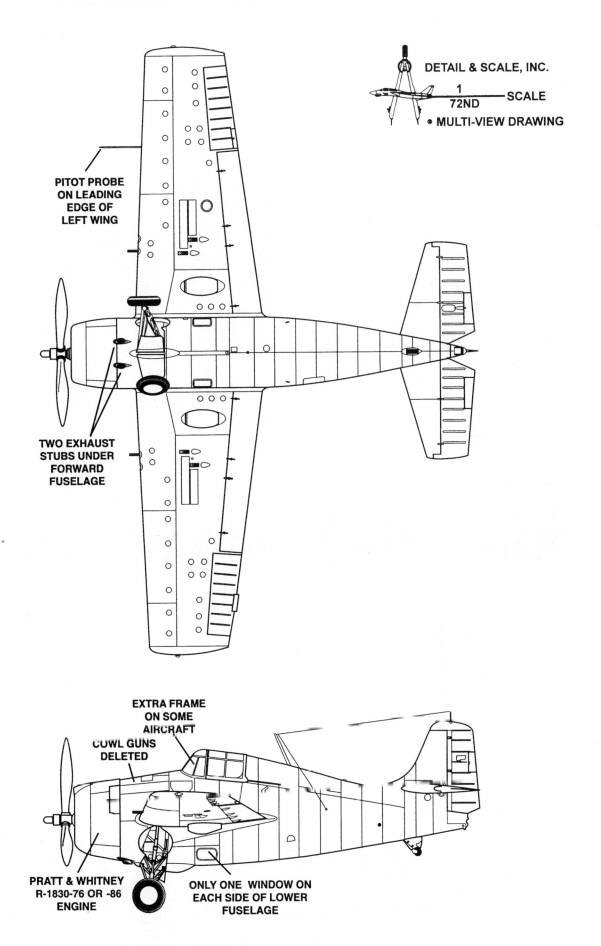

DETAIL & SCALE, INC.

$\dfrac{1}{72ND}$ —— SCALE

● MULTI-VIEW DRAWING

PITOT PROBE
ON LEADING
EDGE OF
LEFT WING

TWO EXHAUST
STUBS UNDER
FORWARD
FUSELAGE

EXTRA FRAME
ON SOME
AIRCRAFT

COWL GUNS
DELETED

PRATT & WHITNEY
R-1830-76 OR -86
ENGINE

ONLY ONE WINDOW ON
EACH SIDE OF LOWER
FUSELAGE

DETAIL & SCALE, 1/72nd SCALE COPYRIGHT © DRAWINGS BY LLOYD S. JONES

F4F-3 COCKPIT DETAILS

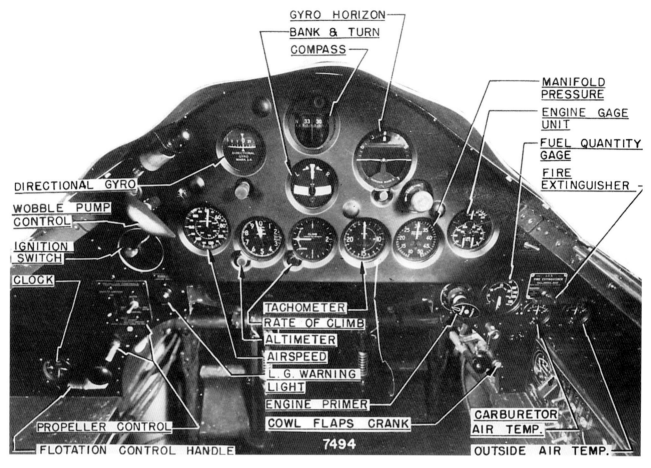

GYRO HORIZON
BANK & TURN
COMPASS
MANIFOLD PRESSURE
ENGINE GAGE UNIT
FUEL QUANTITY GAGE
FIRE EXTINGUISHER
DIRECTIONAL GYRO
WOBBLE PUMP CONTROL
IGNITION SWITCH
CLOCK
TACHOMETER
RATE OF CLIMB
ALTIMETER
AIRSPEED
L.G. WARNING LIGHT
ENGINE PRIMER
COWL FLAPS CRANK
PROPELLER CONTROL
FLOTATION CONTROL HANDLE
CARBURETOR AIR TEMP.
OUTSIDE AIR TEMP.
7494

Above: Features on the instrument panel in an F4F-3 are identified in this photograph provided to the Navy from Grumman. Check these features with those shown in the photographs on pages 40 and 41. Colors are illustrated on those pages. (Grumman)

Below left: Items on the left side of the cockpit are identified in this photograph. Although there were some changes in the cockpit details from one version of the Wildcat to the next, their basic features remained the same, particularly on the sides. The basic color inside the cockpit was Interior Green. (Grumman)

Below right: Details on the right side of the cockpit are identified in this photo, however the radio gear has not been installed. It was usually mounted in the aft area on the right side, and it varied at times depending on where the aircraft operated. (Grumman)

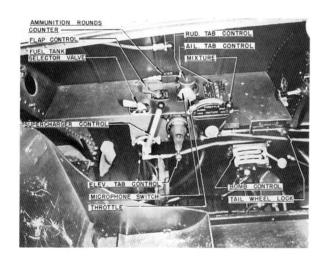

AMMUNITION ROUNDS COUNTER
FLAP CONTROL
FUEL TANK SELECTOR VALVE
RUD. TAB CONTROL
AIL. TAB CONTROL
MIXTURE
SUPERCHARGER CONTROL
ELEV. TAB CONTROL
MICROPHONE SWITCH
THROTTLE
BOMB CONTROL
TAIL WHEEL LOCK

SPARE FUSES & BULBS (UNDER DOOR)
DISTRIBUTION PANEL & SWITCH BOX
STARTER SWITCH
VERY'S PISTOL
L.G. POSITION INDICATOR
L.G. HAND CRANK
RATCHET RELEASE
MAIN TERMINAL BOX
GUN CHARGING HANDLES

ENGINE DETAILS

The cowling used on the first F4F-3s with the R-1830-76 engine is shown here. It has the carburetor scoop at the top of the cowl lip and the two scoops inside the cowling for intercooler air. The propeller is a Curtiss Electric design with a diameter of nine feet, nine inches. This configuration was also used on a few late F4F-3s, F4F-4s, and F4F-7s.

A close-up shows the Pratt & Whitney data plate on the engine's crankcase.

The left scoop for the intercooler air is shown here. It is mounted inside the cowling at the four o'clock position. The inside of the cowling is painted Interior Green.

With the access panels removed, the duct for the intercooler air and other features are visible on the left side of the installed powerplant. (Grumman)

FLOTATION BAGS

Above: Early F4F-3s had flotation bags in the wings that deployed automatically in the event of a ditching at sea. The aircraft could serve as a big life raft for the pilot and then be recovered and salvaged. This photograph was taken during testing of the system at Grumman's plant at Bethpage, New York. (Grumman)

Middle left: In May 1941, Ensign H. E. Tennes deliberately ditched an F4F-3 in San Diego Bay, because he had a damaged landing gear that prevented him from landing ashore. Note the white 6-F-2 fuselage code indicating that this aircraft was assigned to VF-6. It is painted in the overall Light Gray scheme. (NMNA)

Bottom left: The flotation system worked perfectly and the aircraft remained afloat. Ensign Tennes can be seen standing on the left wing next to the cockpit. A crane is about to be attached to the aircraft so that it can be hoisted aboard a ship and taken to a repair facility. On May 28, 1941, shortly after this ditching, this feature was deleted from the production lines to save weight. It was also thought that an aircraft which was ditched in a combat area would just as likely be recovered by the enemy as by friendly forces. (NMNA)

LIFE RAFT DETAILS

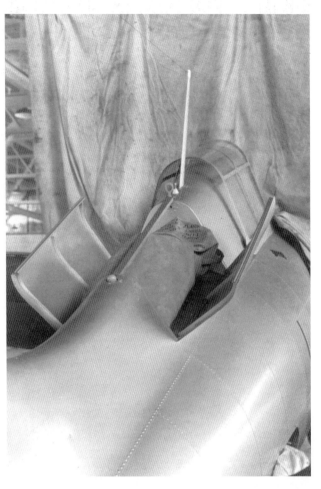

Above left: Wildcats had a life raft stored in the spine of the fuselage behind the cockpit. It was packed in a zippered yellow bag inside the compartment. Here a pilot shows how the bagged raft would be removed from the aircraft. *(Piet collection)*

Above right: Clamshell doors allowed the raft to be removed from either side of the fuselage. *(Grumman)*

Below: The deployed raft is shown inflated next to the aircraft in a factory photograph. After the flotation bags were eliminated, the life raft proved to be impractical in most situations, because the aircraft sank before the raft could be deployed. As a result, a flotation type seat cushion was usually included in the aircraft. *(Grumman)*

ARMAMENT DETAILS

Left: An F4F-3 prepares to take off from USS RANGER, CV-4. A 100-pound bomb is loaded under each wing, and these small bombs were the only external armament carried on the early versions of the Wildcat. Later, 250-pound bombs could be carried, and FM-2s had provisions for six 5-inch rockets. (NMNA)

Below: The F4F-3 had four .50-caliber machine guns mounted in the wings. A total of 1,720 rounds of ammunition were carried, so each weapon had a very ample supply of 430 rounds. These are the two guns in the right wing, and those in the left would be a mirror image of what is shown here. Note how the inboard gun is further forward than the outboard gun. (Grumman)

CANOPY DETAILS

Except for the F4F-7, which had a different windscreen, the windscreen and canopy on all Wildcat variants remained essentially unchanged. The one noticeable exception was the addition frame on each side of the windscreen as seen on the aircraft at the bottom of this page. (Grumman)

A front view provides a good look at the flat bulletproof glass in the windscreen. A small air intake for cockpit ventilation is on top of the windscreen, but this was not on all Wildcats. (Grumman)

Above: Additional details of the sliding canopy are visible in this view from above. Also note that the center section of the fuselage around the cockpit has a constant diameter. Many published drawings of the Wildcat show this incorrectly. (Grumman)

Below: F4F-3, BuNo. 3983, was one of the Wildcats that had the extra frame on each side of the windscreen. Note also that this aircraft was one of the late production F4F-3s that had the four cooling flaps on each side of the cowling, but there was no carburetor scoop on the top of the cowl ring. (Grumman)

FUSELAGE DETAILS

Most F4F-3s had a single cooling flap on each side of the cowling. The fairing on the side of the fuselage just forward of the landing gear first appeared on F4F-3A, BuNo. 3905, and it remained a standard feature on all subsequent F4F-3As and F4F-3s. It was also on the F4F-4, FM-1, and F4F-7, but it was not on the XF4F-8 or the FM-2, both of which had the Wright R-1820 engine.

A close-up shows details of the cooling flap on the left side of the cowling. This single flap proved inadequate for the R-1830 powerplant, and it was discontinued with F4F-3, BuNo. 3969. Beginning with BuNo. 3970, there were four cooling flaps on each side of the cowling, and this arrangement was used on all subsequent variants of the Wildcat that were powered by the R-1830 engine.

The forward end of the antenna wire was anchored to the top of a slanted mast mounted on the spine of the aircraft. On some FM-2s, the mast was vertical, but it was still located in this position just aft of the open canopy. Note the white insulator where the wire attaches to the mast.

The antenna wire entered the aft fuselage on the left side. Antenna wire arrangements differed depending on the types of radios that were carried, but this was the most common configuration. Some Wildcats also had antenna wires running between the tips of their horizontal stabilizers and the fuselage.

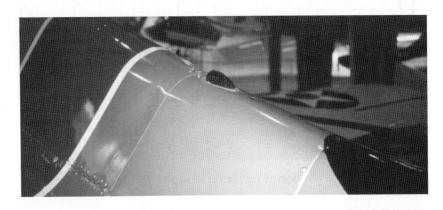

Right: The upper beacon was located on the spine of the fuselage just forward of the vertical tail.

Center left: Access to the radios and other equipment inside the aft fuselage was gained through a hinged panel on the lower right side. This panel was on all Wildcat variants.

Center right: The hook for the catapult bridle was housed in a fairing between the main landing gear doors.

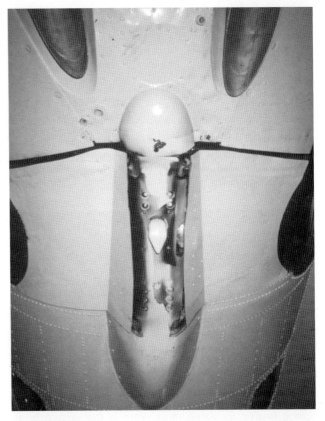

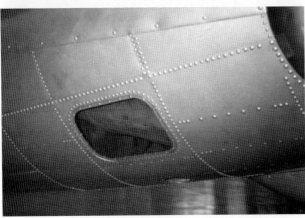

Although the XF4F-2 and XF4F-3 had two windows on each side of the lower fuselage, production Wildcats had only one on each side. These windows provided limited visibility directly below the aircraft.

The windows in the lower fuselage were standard on all variants except the FM-2. Although the openings remained on the FM-2, the clear windows were replaced with solid metal panels.

WING DETAILS

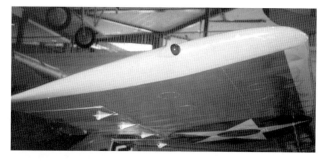

Navigation lights were located on the tip of each wing.

An approach light was located inside the leading edge of the left wing. This approach light has sometimes been misidentified as a landing light or as the gun camera in other publications.

A formation light was on top of each wing near the tip.

Spring loaded tie down rings were in the underside of each wing, and the one under the left wing can be seen here within the national insignia. It is partly in the white star and partly in the red disc.

A small visual flap indicator was on top of the left wing near the trailing edge and the walkway.

The ailerons were covered with fabric, and the left aileron had a trim tab that had an actuator on the top.

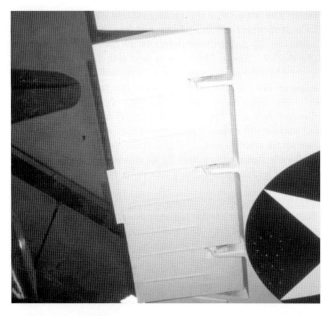

Details of the right aileron are visible in this underside view. Note the three hinges and the fixed balance tab on the trailing edge.

An overall view of the underside of the left wing reveals its simple shape. The locations of the retractable landing light, gun slots, and oil cooler fairing are apparent.

A close-up provides a better look at the retractable landing light. Also note the hinges for the split flap.

A detailed photo provides a close look at the fairing for the oil cooler and the two slots through which expended shells and links were discharged when the guns were fired. This is the underside of the right wing.

Almost the entire trailing edge of each wing was used for the split flaps and ailerons. Three large hinges attached each aileron to the wings, while four hinges were on each flap.

TAIL DETAILS

Left: The aft end of the radio antenna wire was attached to a stub mast on top of the rudder. This remained the same on all production versions of the Wildcat through the F4F-7. Some FM-2s also had this arrangement, but most FM-2s had the antenna wire attached to the leading edge of the vertical stabilizer near the top.

Center, left and right: The design of the tail was established with the final configuration of the XF4F-3, and it remained unchanged until the taller vertical tail and rudder were installed on the XF4F-8 and FM-2. The fabric covered rudder had a trim tab with the actuator on the right side. (Both Grumman)

Bottom: The horizontal tail was located low on the vertical stabilizer, and it had no dihedral. The horizontal stabilizer was mounted with an incidence of + 1.5 degrees. (Grumman)

Like the ailerons and rudder, the elevators were metal framework covered with fabric. Elevators could be deflected twenty-six degrees up and twenty degrees down.

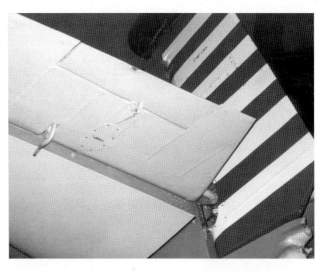

Each elevator had a trim tab, and the one on the left elevator had its actuator on the lower surface. An oval shaped panel allowed access to adjust the tab.

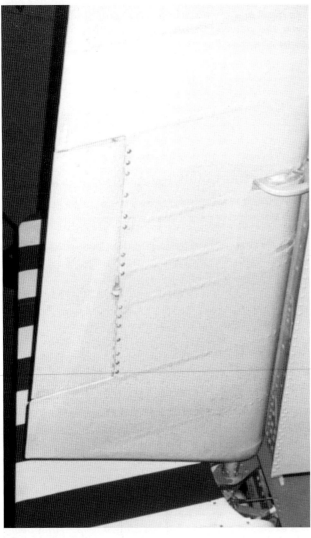

The actuator for the trim tab on the right elevator was on the upper surface, thus allowing the elevators to be used interchangeably between the left and right sides. This is the trim tab on the right elevator as seen from below.

The counterbalances for the elevators were located at the tip. The combined area of the elevators aft of the hinge line was 18.62 square feet.

The arresting hook was housed inside the tail cone. When it was to be used, it slid aft on rails and hung down as the aircraft approached the carrier for landing. The extended hook is illustrated on the next page.

TAIL WHEEL & ARRESTING HOOK DETAILS

The Wildcat was fitted with a fixed tail gear, and the strut assembly was usually covered with an aerodynamic fairing. A hard rubber tire was used for shipboard operations. *(Grumman)*

In this underside view, the aerodynamic fairing has been removed and details of the strut are visible. Also note how the opening in the bottom of the fuselage is the same shape as the cross section of the fairing.

A pneumatic tire was used for operations from land bases. At first, a low pressure tire was used, but beginning in January 1943, a high pressure tire was introduced that could be used aboard carriers as well as from land. *(Grumman)*

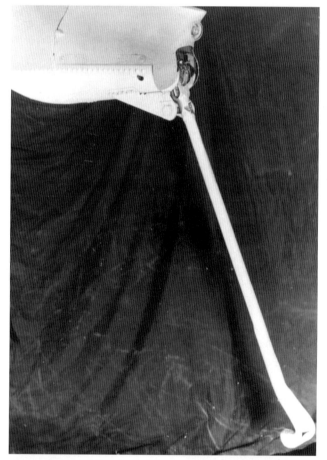

The extended arresting hook is shown here. After being moved aft from its stowed position inside the tail, it hung down at this angle until it engaged one of the arresting wires on the carrier. Also note the clear light on the tail cone. *(Grumman)*

COLOR GALLERY

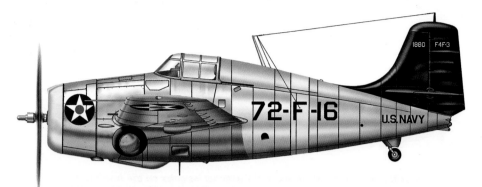

Early production F4F-3s were delivered in the Navy's colorful pre-war paint schemes that were used through 1940. This aircraft was assigned to VF-72, aboard the USS WASP, CV-7.

On December 30, 1940, the Navy issued a directive that specified an overall Light Gray (FS 36440) paint scheme to reduce the aircraft's visibility in the event of hostilities. This F4F-3 was assigned to VF-71 at NAS Norfolk, Virginia, in the spring of 1941.

The overall Light Gray scheme was officially replaced with the Non-specular Blue Gray over Non-specular Light Gray paint scheme in October 1941. Red and white stripes were painted on the rudder. This F4F-3 was assigned to VF-6 aboard USS ENTER-PRISE, CV-6, in March 1942, and it has the oversized fuselage insignia.

On May 20, 1942, the Navy ordered the removal of the red disc from the national insignia and the red and white stripes from the rudder to prevent confusion with the red Japanese insignia. This F4F-4 was assigned to VGF-29 aboard the USS SANTEE, CVE-29.

A yellow surround was added to the national insignias on the fuselage and under the wings of U. S. aircraft that participated in the invasion of North Africa. This F4F-4 was assigned to VF-9 aboard USS RANGER, CV-4, for Operation Torch in November 1942.

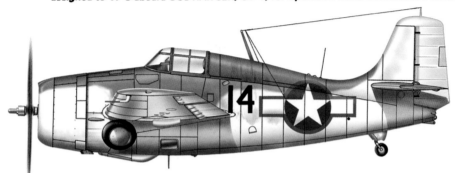

A Dark Gull Gray over white paint scheme was adopted for aircraft operating in the North Atlantic, including Wildcats and Avengers aboard the escort carriers of the Atlantic Fleet. This FM-1 was assigned to VC-55 aboard USS BLOCK ISLAND, CVE-21.

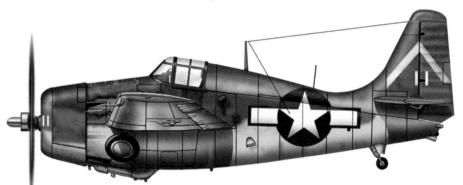

The tri-color scheme of Sea Blue, Intermediate Blue, and white was used from 1943 through 1944. This FM-2 was assigned to VC-80 which operated from USS MANILA BAY, CVE-61.

On March 22, 1944, the Navy directed that all carrier based fighters operating in the Pacific would be painted in an overall Glossy Sea Blue scheme, however it took several months for this to be fully implemented. This FM-2 was assigned to VC-88 aboard USS HOGGATT BAY, CVE-75, and it was named "Hot Lips."

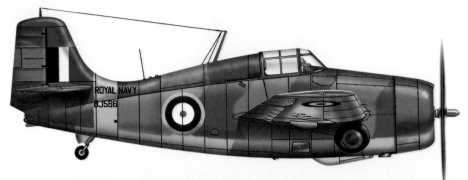

A camouflage pattern of Extra Dark Sea Gray and Dark Slate Gray was applied to Martlet Is operating in the Great Britain in late 1941. The undersides and aft fuselage band were the British Sky color.

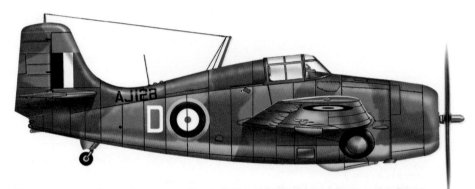

The same camouflage scheme was also applied to this Martlet II which flew from Royal Navy carriers in the Indian Ocean during operations against Madagascar in 1942.

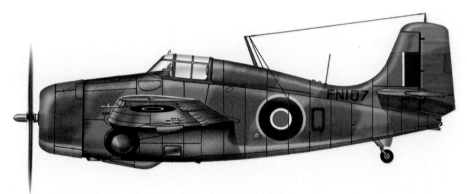

This Martlet IV was assigned to the HMS Victorious during September 1942.

By the end of the war, British Wildcat VIs were painted in the U. S. Navy's overall Glossy Sea Blue Scheme. This aircraft operated with the Royal Navy's Far East Fleet.

WILDCAT COLORS

Top: Three F4F-3s from VF-5 fly together during the summer of 1941. They are painted in the overall Nonspecular Light Gray (FS 36440) scheme which was ordered into use in February 1941. They also have fuselage insignias which are one-half the standard size. The fuselage codes are flat white letters and numbers that are twelve inches high.   (Piet collection)

Middle: Like the Navy, the Marines also used twelve-inch high letters and numbers on the sides of the fuselage to indicate the unit, type of aircraft, and the aircraft's number within the squadron. This F4F-3 is from VMF-121.   (Piet collection)

Below: During the war games in November 1941, F4F-3As from VMF-111 were among the participants. Crosses on the wings and fuselage indicate that these Wildcats were part of the red force. This photograph is reproduced here as large as possible, because it provides an excellent look at the underside details on an F4F-3A. These Marine aircraft have the larger pneumatic tire on the tail gear that was used for operations from land bases.   (Piet collection)

On October 13, 1941, a new directive was issued that changed the official paint scheme once again. All surfaces viewed from above and the sides were painted Non-specular Blue-Gray, while the undersides were painted Non-specular Light Gray. U. S. Navy fighters were seldom given names, but this F4F-4 was an exception that was named ROSENBLATT'S "REPLY."

(National Archives)

In the Atlantic, a Dark Gull Gray over white scheme was adopted for aircraft assigned to the escort carriers that protected the convoys moving between the United States and England. This is an FM-2 aboard the USS CHARGER, CVE-30 on May 8, 1944. The escort carriers usually operated a composite squadron of FM-1s or FM-2s and TBM Avengers. Both aircraft were Grumman designs that were built by the Eastern Aircraft Division of General Motors. (Piet collection)

Typical flight gear worn by U. S. Navy and Marine pilots while flying Wildcats in the tropical Southwest Pacific climates included a khaki flight suit, cloth or leather helmet with headphones and goggles, and a Mae West life vest. (Piet collection)

The camouflage pattern on the first Martlet I is visible in this high view. This aircraft was originally part of the French order, and it still has the original red, white, and blue stripes on the rudder. The propeller was highly polished natural metal. (Piet collection)

LANDING GEAR DETAILS & COLORS

On Wildcats that were delivered in the colorful prewar schemes, the main landing gear, including the wheels, struts, and interior of the well, was painted with the same silver color as the fuselage. The two doors attached to the lower strut assemblies were also painted silver on all surfaces.

The landing gear on camouflaged Wildcats was usually painted the same color as the underside of the fuselage, but many had part of the landing gear painted black as shown here. Aircraft in the Dark Gull Gray over white scheme had part of the struts, the inside of the doors, and the interior of the well painted a medium gray color.

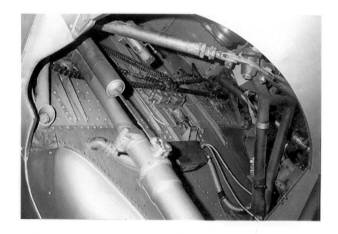

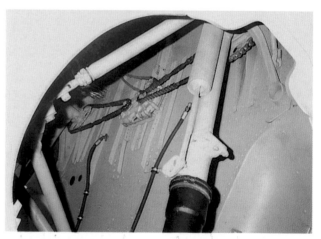

Details inside the main gear well are shown here from the right side. The view looks up and slightly aft through the opening for the right wheel, and the chains that operated the landing gear can be seen on the bulkhead.

This photograph was taken through the opening for the left wheel on the same aircraft shown directly above. The pilot manually turned a crank that retracted or lowered the gear through a series of chains and gears.

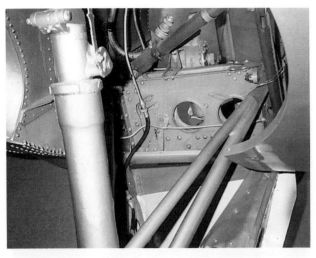

Structural strength for the lower part of the landing gear assembly was provided by a drag link support structure that extended between the openings for the two main wheels. Note the lightening holes in the structure.

A fuel pump and strainer were located on the left side of the drag link support structure. Note the fuel line running into the pump from the main fuel tank within the fuselage.

Hydraulic lines for the brakes ran down each strut assembly to the inside of the wheels.

Details on the inside of the left main landing gear wheel are visible in this close-up.

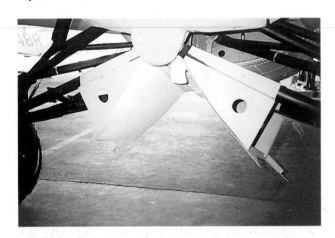

When the gear was retracted, the bottom part of the gear well was covered by doors attached to the lower strut assemblies. The hook for the catapult bridle can be seen between the two doors.

In this view, the gear is retracted. The wheels and tires cover the circular opening of the well, while the doors cover the lower part. Again note the hook for the catapult bridle in the faring under the fuselage.

F4F-3 COCKPIT DETAILS & COLORS

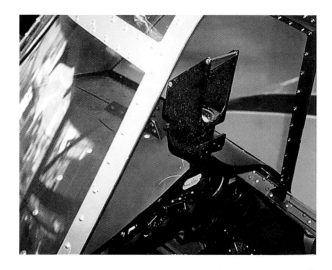

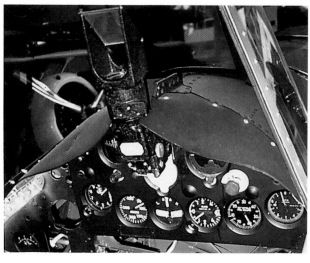

For many years, there were no restored examples of F4F-3 Wildcats. However, the National Museum of Naval Aviation in Pensacola, Florida, now has an F4F-3 and an F4F-3A that have been painstakingly restored to original condition as accurately as possible. The photographs on this page were taken in the cockpit of the F4F-3. This is the electrical gun sight that replaced the telescopic sight used in the XF4F-3s.

The directional gyro is missing above the turn and bank indicator, but otherwise the instrument panel is complete. The panel was flat black, as were the left console and boxes on the right side, but the basic color inside the cockpit was Interior Green.

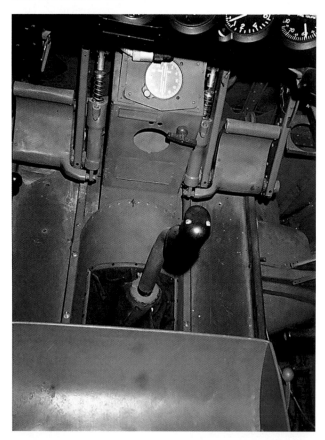

The throttle quadrant and trim wheels were on the left side of the cockpit. The silver handle is the supercharger control, while the levers on the smaller quadrant mounted low on the cockpit side are the bomb release handles. The red switch behind the supercharger control lever is the fuel tank selector valve.

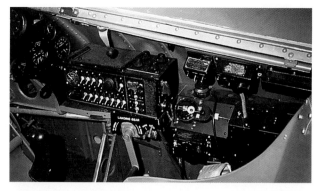

The cockpit did not have a solid floor. The pilot's feet rested against the rudder pedals which were mounted above troughs. The control column was on a hump at the center of the cockpit. The cockpit was open on either side of the foot troughs, thus allowing the pilot to see down through the windows in the lower fuselage.

The electrical distribution box was the main feature on the right side of the cockpit. The crank that raised and lowered the main landing gear was mounted next to the pilot's leg, and radio controls were located further aft on the right side. Also note the gages on the auxiliary panel just forward of the electrical distribution box.

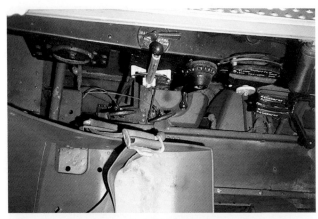

This view looks down into the lower fuselage on the left side of the cockpit. Two red gun charging handles are visible, as is the lower window.

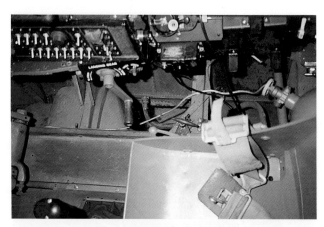

Two gun charging handles are on the right side, although only one can be seen in this view. The green bottle contains breathing oxygen for the pilot.

The seat in the Wildcat was a simple metal design with a framework that mounted inside the cockpit. Early Wildcats did not have shoulder harnesses, but these were added later.

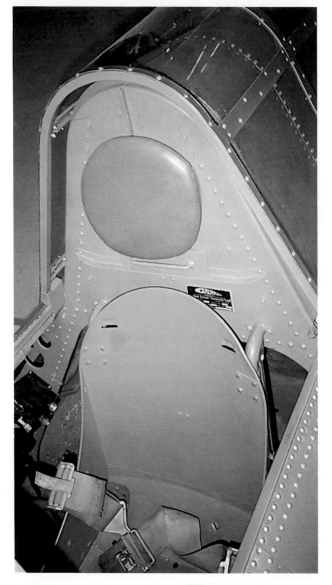

A padded headrest was above the seat on the aft cockpit bulkhead. It was circular in shape and could be tan, dark brown, or black. Note the Grumman manufacturer's plate just behind the top of the seat.

F4F-4 COCKPIT DETAILS & COLORS

Above left: The reflector gun sight used in the F4F-4 and FM-1 is shown here in this beautifully restored F4F-4 on display at the Marine Corps Museum at Quantico, Virginia. Note the pad on the rear edge of the sight. It helped to lessen the blow to the pilot's head if he was thrown forward against it.

Above right: The instrument panel is complete except for the turn and bank indicator that is missing near the center of the panel at the bottom. The hole beneath the radio compass on the center console was for cabin ventilation air. The orange dots on some of the instruments are small stickers that were added after the instruments were checked to insure that there was no radiation from their luminous dials. They were not on operational aircraft. Note the instruments on the auxiliary panel to the right of the main panel.

The items on the left console were essentially the same as those found in the F4F-3, but note that the console is not painted flat black. The large white item next to the seat is the landing gear warning horn.

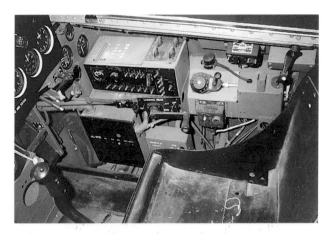

The electrical distribution box, landing gear crank, and radio controls remained the primary items on the right side of the cockpit. Circuit breaker reset buttons are on the large lower panel.

This F4F-4 has a dark brown headrest, but otherwise it is the same as that found in the F4F-3. Seats were usually painted Interior Green, but it was not unusual to find black seats in Wildcats.

R-1830 DETAILS & COLORS

Above left: The F4F-3, F4F-4, and FM-1 variants of the Wildcat were all powered by versions of Pratt & Whitney's R-1830, twin row, radial engine. This front view shows the details of the engine as installed in late F4F-3s, F4F-4s, and FM-1s. This arrangement had the scoop at the top of the cowl ring and the two scoops inside the ring at the four and eight o'clock positions.

Above right: This R-1830 is on display at the National Museum of Naval Aviation, and it has been cut in half vertically to reveal the inner details of the powerplant.

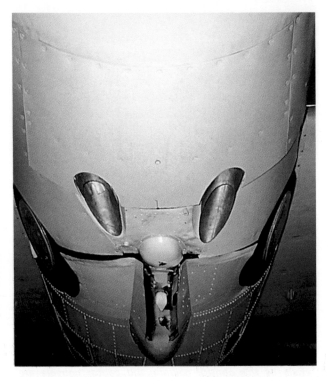

A rear view shows the black accessories on the aft end of the R-1830. The downdraft carburetor is the large item at the top.

The exhaust from the engine was routed through a manifold to two stubs located at the aft end of the cowling beneath the fuselage.

FM-2 COCKPIT DETAILS & COLORS

The instrument panel in the FM-2 was slightly different from that found in earlier variants of the Wildcat, but the basic layout and features were very similar. The red handle to the right controls the position of the cowl flaps.

A Mark VIII illuminated gun sight was standard in the FM-2. Compare this unit to the gun sights used in the F4F-3 and F4F-4 as illustrated on pages 40 and 42 respectively.

Features on the left side of the cockpit remained the same as they had on previous versions. They included the throttle quadrant with the engine controls, trim wheels, supercharger handle, and fuel selector switch. The small red handle just aft of the rudder trim tab knob is the flap control.

Details of the control column and center console are shown here. On the FM-2, a control valve for the cabin ventilation air was added inside the hole in the center stand.

The right side of the cockpit in the FM-2 was essentially unchanged from what was installed in the preceding variants. Even this final version of the Wildcat had a manual crank to raise and lower the main landing gear.

Above left and right: The FM-2 retained the floorless cockpit with the open areas on each side of the foot troughs. However, the windows in the lower fuselage were deleted, so there was no visibility beneath the aircraft.

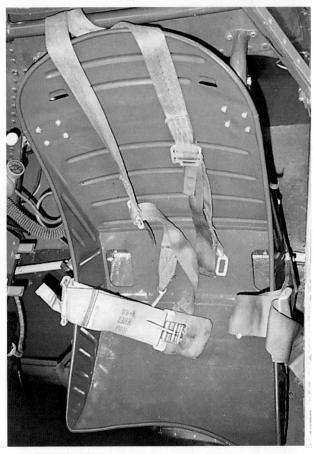

The headrest also remained unchanged from that found in previous variants of the Wildcat, and in this case, the covering is flat black. Note the Interior Green color on the inside surfaces of the canopy's framework.

Details of the lap belts and the shoulder harness straps are visible in this view of a seat in an FM-2. Like most other features in the cockpit, the seat was the same as used in all earlier Wildcats.

FM-2 DETAILS IN COLOR

The major change on the FM-2 was the use of a Wright R-1820, single row, radial engine. This powerplant required more exhaust stubs than the Pratt & Whitney R-1830. Two stubs were located above the wing on the left side of the fuselage beneath the trailing edge of the cowling.

Three exhaust stubs were positioned above the wing on the right side of the fuselage. Like the two stubs on the left, they discharged the exhaust from beneath the trailing edge of the cowling. The R-1820 engine also allowed a change back to a single cowl flap on each side instead of four as used on the F4F-4 and FM-1.

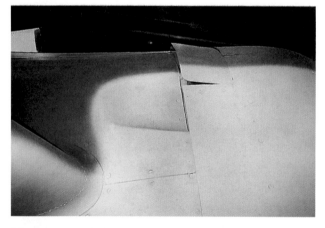

There was an indented area on each side of the forward fuselage to provide clearance for the exhaust that was discharged from the upper exhaust stubs. This is the indented area on the right side of a freshly painted aircraft, but the exhaust burned away much of the paint along the sides of the fuselage on operational FM-2s.

Additional exhaust stubs were located under the trailing edge of the cowling beneath the fuselage. They vented the exhaust past two indented areas between the main landing gear. Each area had two exhaust stubs. This brought the total to nine stubs, one for each cylinder. Note the burned areas aft of the exhausts.

Above left: FM-2s had two .50-caliber machine guns mounted in each wing, and the inboard gun was positioned a little further forward than the outboard gun. As a result, its muzzle extended a little past the leading edge of the wing. These are the gun ports on the right wing, and the photograph was taken when the wing was in the folded position.

Above right: To increase the firepower of the FM-2, three zero-length rocket launchers were mounted under each wing. These were used to carry 5-inch rockets.

Right: Three identification lights were located under the aft fuselage. They were red, green, and amber, from front to rear.

To counter the increased torque of the R-1820 engine, the FM-2 had a taller vertical tail and more rudder area than previous Wildcats. The rudder had a trim tab with the actuator on the right side.

Like the earlier variants, some FM-2s had a stub mast for the antenna wire at the top of the rudder as shown here, while others had the antenna wire attached to the leading edge of the vertical stabilizer.

WRIGHT R-1820 DETAILS & COLORS

Above left: The Wright R-1820 engine had only one row of nine cylinders, and therefore a shorter cowling could be used than that required by the Pratt & Whitney R-1830 with its two rows of cylinders. Unlike the earlier versions of the Wildcat, the FM-2 had no intakes in the lip of the cowling. Instead, air was taken in through the four black intakes mounted between the lower cylinders.

Above right: This Wright R-1820 has certain components cut away to reveal the internal details of the powerplant. It is on display at the National Museum of Naval Aviation at Pensacola, Florida. Although the R-1820 had less displacement and five less cylinders, it provided 160 more horsepower than the Pratt & Whitney R-1830.

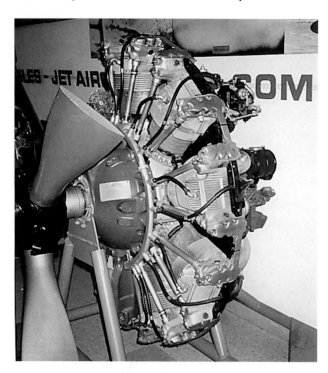

The crankcase and the details on the front of the cylinders are visible in this photograph. Note the two black spark plug wires for each cylinder.

A left side view provides a look at the exhaust manifold behind the cylinders and the black carburetor on top of the engine.

F4F-3S WILDCATFISH

Top: F4F-3, BuNo. 4038, was modified to a floatplane configuration and redesignated the F4F-3S. Called the Wildcatfish, it was one of several types of Navy aircraft to be fitted and evaluated with floats. These projects were carried out because the Navy was concerned that it might not have enough carriers or bases in the Pacific from which its aircraft could operate. Fortunately, America's industrial might produced carriers at a rapid rate, and the Navy's construction battalions (CBs) proved they could transform jungles into airfields practically over night. As a result, the floatplane version of the Wildcat was not put into production.   (Grumman)

Middle right: The first flight of the F4F-3S was made by test pilot F. T. Kurt on February 28, 1943. The large fin under the rear fuselage was not present during early trials.   (NMNA)

Bottom right: Auxiliary vertical rudders were added to the horizontal tail surfaces to solve problems with yaw stability caused by the large Edo floats. They were linked to work together with the main rudder. A large fin was subsequently added under the aft fuselage.   (NMNA)

XF4F-4

Above: The new monoplanes were larger than the previous biplanes, and this meant that fewer of them could be stored aboard an aircraft carrier. It was quickly realized that folding wings would permit a considerably larger number of aircraft to be fitted on the limited space aboard ship. As a result, hydraulically folding wings were installed on F4F-3, BuNo. 1897, and it became the XF4F-4. It retained the long pitot probe on the leading edge of the left wing.   (Grumman)

Middle left: Unlike other manufacturers who simply designed wings to fold up above the aircraft along a straight hinge line, Grumman used an S-shaped hinge line and designed the wings to twist as they folded back along the sides of the fuselage. This kept the height of the folded wing to a minimum. The design was also used on Grumman's F6F Hellcat and TBF Avenger as well. The wings are shown here in an intermediate position as they are folded back along the sides of the fuselage.   (Grumman)

Bottom left: A view from behind the XF4F-4 shows how the folded wings reduced the width of the aircraft to that of the horizontal stabilizers while not increasing the overall height. For a detailed look at the wing fold hinge and joint on production Wildcats, see pages 58 and 59.   (Grumman)

F4F-4

Grumman built 1,169 F4F-4s. These Wildcats had folding wings, but unlike the XF4F-4, they were operated manually instead of hydraulically. Armament was increased to six .50-caliber machine guns, although this change was met with displeasure by most pilots. The long pitot probe was replaced with a short one under the left wing tip. (National Archives)

Following the 285 F4F-3s and 95 F4F-3As, 1,169 F4F-4s were built by Grumman. Five were produced in 1941, while the remaining 1,164 were completed in 1942. These would be the final production Wildcats built by Grumman with the subsequent variants being delivered by the Eastern Aircraft Division of General Motors.

The F4F-4 was powered by the Pratt & Whitney R-1830-86 engine used in late F4F-3s, and the four cooling flaps on each side of the cowling became standard. But the F4F-4s had two major differences from the previous F4F-3 and F4F-3A. First, folding wings were installed, but unlike the hydraulically operated wings in the XF4F-4, these were manually operated. The long pitot probe, located on the leading edge of the left wing on the F4F-3

and F4F-3A, was replaced by a small probe under the tip of the left wing. This change was made because the longer probe could be damaged when the wing folded.

The second change on the F4F-4 was an increase in firepower with the addition of two more .50-caliber machine guns in the wings, thus bringing the total to six. The additional gun in each wing was located much further outboard than the other two, and the inboard gun, although mounted forward of the center gun, no longer extended beyond the leading edge of the wing.

Although the two additional guns increased the firepower by fifty percent, this was not welcomed by many pilots, because the firing time was substantially reduced. The Wildcat variants with four guns carried a total of 1,720 rounds of ammunition or 430 rounds per gun. In the F4F-4, only 1,440 rounds were carried, which meant there were only 240 rounds per gun. Pilots almost unani-

An F4F-4 prepares to launch from USS RANGER, CV-4, during Operation Torch. Note the addition of the outboard gun in each wing and the approach light outboard of the inboard two guns on the left wing. (NMNA)

Guns on F4F-4s aboard USS RANGER are test fired before going into action. Note that VF-9's aircraft have fuselage codes, while VF-41's Wildcats have only the aircraft number on the sides of the fuselage. Aircraft in Operation Torch had a yellow surround around the national insignias located on the fuselage sides and under the wings. A color profile of 9 F 9 appears on page 34.
(National Archives)

mously preferred the longer firing time available with the four machine guns rather than the increased firepower of the six guns. They reasoned that the lightly constructed Japanese aircraft could easily be destroyed with four guns, and inexperienced pilots, whose marksmanship might not be all that good, needed more time to train their tracers onto their target. As a result, the F4F-4 was the only American variant of the Wildcat to have six guns. The subsequent FM-1 and FM-2 returned to the four-gun arrangement.

With two 58-gallon fuel tanks under its wings, an F4F-4 prepares to launch from the diagonal catapult aboard USS LONG ISLAND, ACV-1, on March 6, 1943. The ship was redesignated CVE-1 in July 1943.
(NMNA)

An F4F-4A version of the Wildcat with the R-1830-90 powerplant was planned for the same reason that the F4F-3A was built, but the reliability of the two-stage, two-speed R-1830-86 engine had been established by this time. As a result, the F4F-4A was never built. A total of 220 F4F-4Bs were delivered to the Royal Navy as Martlet IVs. These were the same as U. S. Navy F4F-4s except that they were powered by a Wright R-1820-40B engine rather than the Pratt & Whitney R-1830-86. They were also fitted with a Hamilton Standard propeller instead of the Curtiss Electric propeller that was installed on F4F-4s.

DATA

Version	F4F-4
Grumman Model Number	G-36B
Number Built	1,169
Armament	6 X .50-caliber machine guns
Powerplant	Pratt & Whitney R-1830-86
Horsepower	1,200
Maximum Speed	318 mph at 19,400
Cruising Speed	190 mph
Initial Rate of Climb	2,190 feet-per-minute
Ceiling	33,700 feet
Maximum Range	1,275 miles
Combat Range	830 miles
Wingspan	38 feet
Length	28 feet, 10.5 inches
Height	11 feet, 9 inches
Empty Weight	5,766 pounds
Gross Weight	7,964 pounds
Maximum Take-off Weight	8,762 pounds
Maximum Internal Fuel	144 gallons
External Fuel	2 X 58-gallon tanks

As he lands, a pilot flairs his F4F-4 Wildcat just above the flight deck of USS COPAHEE, CVE-12, on August 24, 1942. *(NMNA)*

This F4F-4P is painted in the tri-color camouflage scheme of Dark Sea Blue, Intermediate Blue, and white. 2 D 6 is painted in white on the side of the fuselage. *(NMNA)*

Tugs tow F4F-4s of VF-9 to a new position on the flight deck of USS RANGER. *(NMNA)*

Much of the time it was simply muscle power that re-spotted aircraft aboard ship. *(NMNA)*

F4F-4 1/72nd SCALE DRAWINGS

DETAIL & SCALE, INC.

$$\frac{1}{72ND}$$ SCALE

⊛ FIVE-VIEW DRAWING

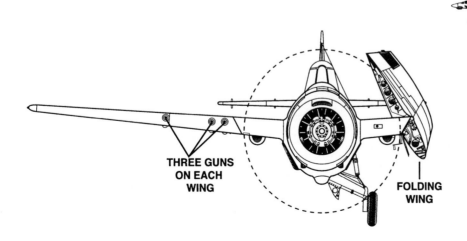

THREE GUNS
ON EACH
WING

FOLDING
WING

DETAIL & SCALE, 1/72nd SCALE COPYRIGHT © DRAWINGS BY LLOYD S. JONES

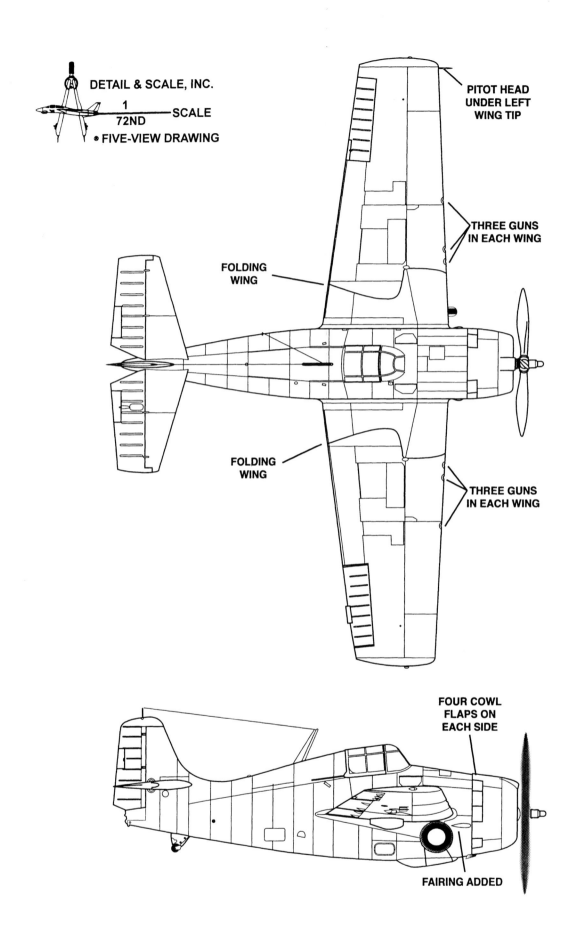

DETAIL & SCALE, INC.

$\frac{1}{72ND}$ ——— SCALE

⊕ FIVE-VIEW DRAWING

PITOT HEAD
UNDER LEFT
WING TIP

THREE GUNS
IN EACH WING

FOLDING
WING

FOLDING
WING

THREE GUNS
IN EACH WING

FOUR COWL
FLAPS ON
EACH SIDE

FAIRING ADDED

DETAIL & SCALE, 1/72nd SCALE COPYRIGHT © DRAWINGS BY LLOYD S. JONES

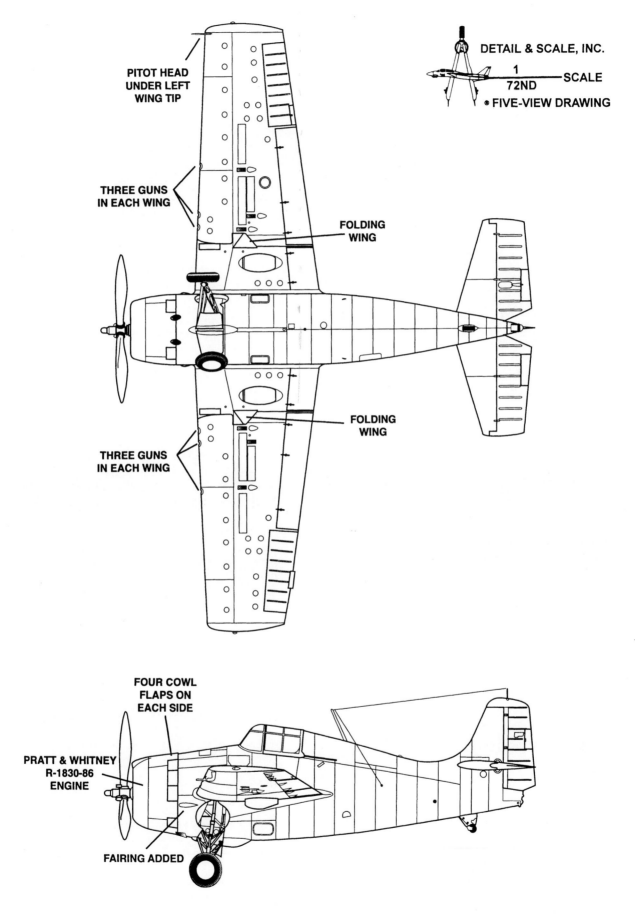

PITOT HEAD
UNDER LEFT
WING TIP

THREE GUNS
IN EACH WING

FOLDING
WING

THREE GUNS
IN EACH WING

FOLDING
WING

DETAIL & SCALE, INC.
1
——— SCALE
72ND
⊛ FIVE-VIEW DRAWING

FOUR COWL
FLAPS ON
EACH SIDE

PRATT & WHITNEY
R-1830-86
ENGINE

FAIRING ADDED

DETAIL & SCALE, 1/72nd SCALE COPYRIGHT © DRAWINGS BY LLOYD S. JONES

F4F-4 DETAILS

F4F-4 COCKPIT DETAILS

1. CLOCK
2. CYLINDER HEAD TEMPERATURE GAGE
3. RUDDER PEDAL ADJUSTMENT LEVER
4. PROPELLER CONTROL
5. IGNITION SWITCH
6. GUN SIGHT LIGHT SWITCH
7. EMERGENCY ELECTRIC FUEL PUMP SWITCH
8. CHECK-OFF SWITCH
9. WINDSHIELD DEFROSTER
10. ALTIMETER
11. DIRECTIONAL GYRO
12. PADDED ELECTRIC GUN SIGHT MOUNT
13. AIRSPEED INDICATOR

14. TURN & BANK INDICATOR
15. RATE OF CLIMB INDICATOR
16. GYRO HORIZON
17. MANIFOLD PRESSURE GAGE
18. TACHOMETER
19. OUTSIDE AIR TEMPERATURE
20. FUEL QUANTITY GAGE
21. PRIMER PUMP
22. COWL FLAPS HANDCRANK
23. ENGINE GAGE UNIT
24. COMPASS
25. OIL DILUTION SWICH
26. RADIO SIGNAL LIGHT

Features on the instrument panel of an F4F-4 are identified in this photograph.   (Grumman)

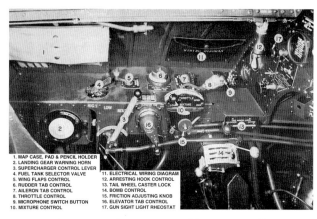

1. MAP CASE, PAD & PENCIL HOLDER
2. LANDING GEAR WARNING HORN
3. SUPERCHARGER CONTROL LEVER
4. FUEL TANK SELECTOR VALVE
5. WING FLAPS CONTROL
6. RUDDER TAB CONTROL
7. AILERON TAB CONTROL
8. THROTTLE CONTROL
9. MICROPHONE SWITCH BUTTON
10. MIXTURE CONTROL
11. ELECTRICAL WIRING DIAGRAM
12. ARRESTING HOOK CONTROL
13. TAIL WHEEL CASTER LOCK
14. BOMB CONTROL
15. FRICTION ADJUSTING KNOB
16. ELEVATOR TAB CONTROL
17. GUN SIGHT LIGHT RHEOSTAT

Details on the left side are named here.   (Grumman)

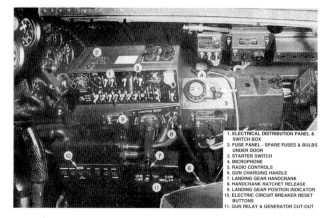

1. ELECTRICAL DISTRIBUTION PANEL & SWITCH BOX
2. FUSE PANEL - SPARE FUSES & BULBS UNDER DOOR
3. STARTER SWITCH
4. MICROPHONE
5. RADIO CONTROLS
6. GUN CHARGING HANDLE
7. LANDING GEAR HANDCRANK
8. HANDCRANK RATCHET RELEASE
9. LANDING GEAR POSITION INDICATOR
10. ELECTRIC CIRCUIT BREAKER RESET BUTTONS
11. GUN RELAY & GENERATOR CUT-OUT

Right side details are labeled in this view.   (Grumman)

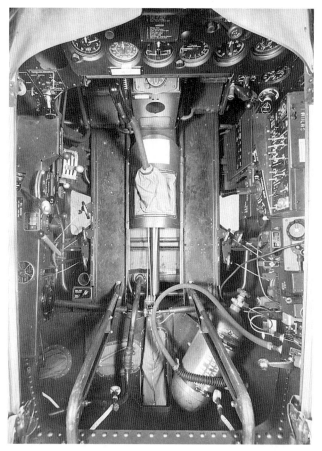

This view looks straight down into the cockpit and reveals the control column, foot troughs, and the windows in the lower fuselage. With the seat removed, the oxygen bottle for the pilot is also visible.   (Grumman)

AFT FUSELAGE DETAILS

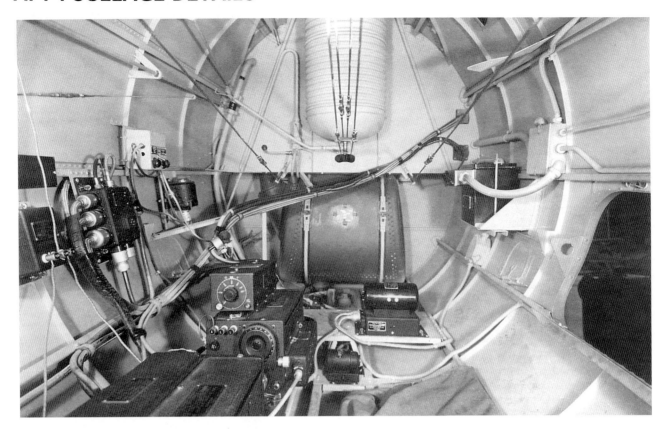

Above: The reserve fuel tank, which held twenty-seven gallons, and some of the radio gear are visible inside the forward end of the aft fuselage compartment of an F4F-4. Access to the compartment was gained through an opening on the right side of the fuselage, and it is visible at the far right side of this photograph. (Grumman)

Below: This view looks to the rear of the same compartment. Note where the radio antenna wire enters the compartment above the radios. A tube ran through the aft end of the compartment, and a bar could be placed through the tube from outside the aircraft and used to lift the rear of the aircraft for servicing. (Grumman)

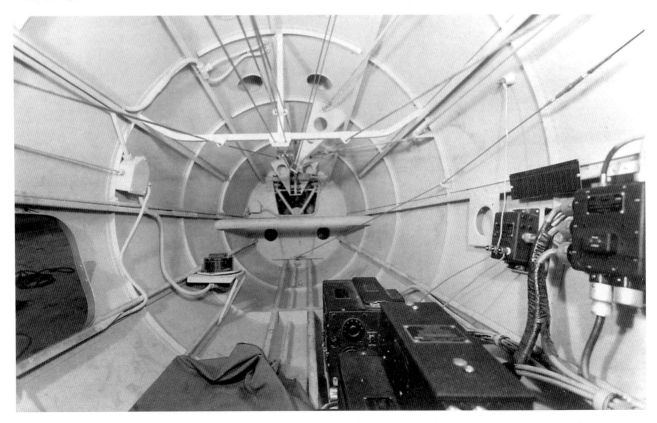

WING FOLD DETAILS

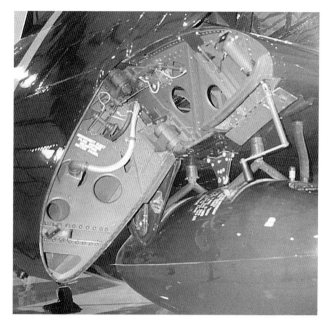

The F4F-4, and all subsequent versions of the Wildcat except the F4F-7, had wings that folded manually. This is the forward end of the wing fold on the right wing, and the handle which locked and unlocked the folding mechanism is visible above the auxiliary fuel tank.

Details of the forward end of the left wing fold are shown here. Note the small door that is open to permit use of the locking handle. The handle was stored up inside the wing when not in use, and the door was closed over it. *(Grumman)*

The left wing joint and hinge line is shown here from behind with the wings folded.

The rear of the right wing hinge line was simply a mirror image of the one on the left.

The long pitot probe used on the F4F-3 and F4F-3A could be easily damaged on the folding wing, so it was replaced with a small probe under the left wing tip on the F4F-4. It remained standard on all subsequent versions of the Wildcat.

An eye was located next to the pitot probe, and one end of a bar or cable could be attached to it. The other end of the cable or bar would be attached to a similar eye on the leading edge of the left horizontal stabilizer, and it would help hold the wing in the folded position when the aircraft was stored.

This front view shows the details inside the break line on the outer panel of the left wing. The one on the outer right wing panel would be exactly the opposite of what is shown here.

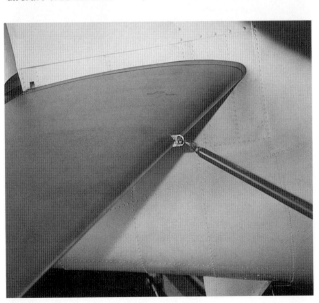

This close-up provides a look at the eye on the leading edge of the right horizontal stabilizer with the bar in place.

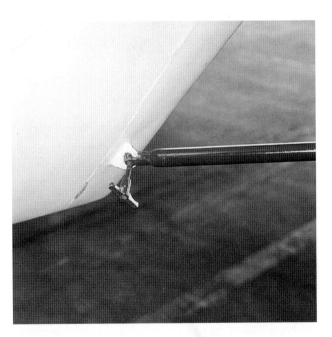

The other end of this bar was attached to an eye on the tip of the right wing near the leading edge, and it held the wing in the folded position.

ARMAMENT DETAILS

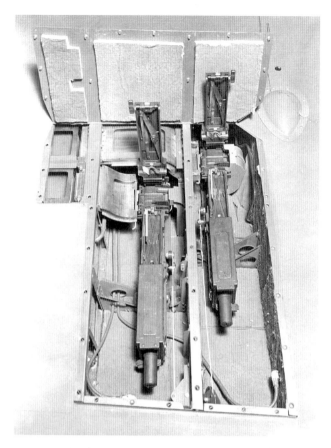

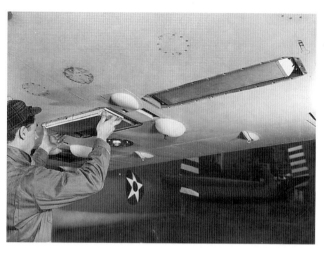

Above left: The two inboard guns in the left wing of an F4F-4 were staggered with the inboard gun located further forward. However, unlike on the F4F-3, F4F-3A, and FM-2, the muzzle of the inboard gun did not extend beyond the leading edge of the wing. (Grumman)

Above right: The two ammunition boxes for the inboard guns were loaded up through a large opening under the wing. The box for the outer gun was also loaded from beneath the wing, and it is seen in place in this photograph. Flat metal access panels covered the boxes once they were in place. This same photograph was identified as being on an F4F-3 in another publication, but the fact that the outboard gun is present indicates that this can only be an F4F-4. (Grumman)

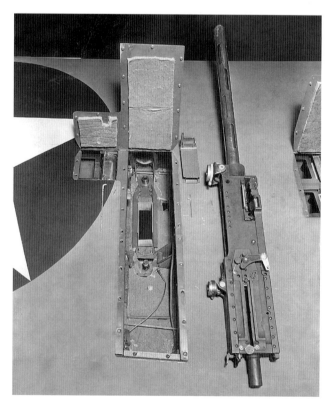

The outboard left gun is visible here. Note the small door outboard of the gun. This permitted the end of the ammunition belt to be loaded into the weapon. (Grumman)

With the gun removed, details inside the bay are visible. Note the slot through which spent shells and links were ejected from the aircraft. (Grumman)

EXTERNAL STORES

Above left: In addition to small bombs, the only other external store usually carried beneath the Wildcat's wings were 58-gallon fuel tanks. These tanks were carried further inboard than the bombs, and on versions with folding wings, they were located on the non-folding, fixed center, section. This is the tank under the right wing of an F4F-4.

Above right: A front view of the tank under the left wing shows just how close the tank was to the fuselage.

A close-up shows the two inverted Y-shaped anti-sway braces for the auxiliary fuel tank. A fuel line near the forward end of the tank runs between the tank and the underside of the wing. The small tapered rack that holds the tank to the wing can be seen about midway between the two braces.

On rare occasions, stores other than bombs were carried on the racks beneath the outer wing panels. In this case, a target release banner is on the standard bomb rack. It was towed behind the Wildcat on a long cable, and it was used for target practice by other pilots or by gunners on the ground or aboard ship.

XF4F-5 & XF4F-6

Above: The fourth and fifth F4F-3s, BuNos. 1846 and 1847, were used as test aircraft with the Wright R-1820-40 engine. These tests were necessary, because the R-1820-40 was the powerplant intended for use in the French Wildcats ordered in 1940. The R-1820 had only one row of cylinders, therefore the cowling was shorter than that used on Wildcats powered by the Pratt & Whitney R-1830 which had two rows of cylinders. (NMNA)

Below: One Wildcat was fitted with the Pratt & Whitney R-1830-90 engine which had a single-stage, two-speed supercharger. It was originally designated the XF4F-6, and it was assigned BuNo. 7031. Subsequently, the designation was changed to XF4F-3A. The R-1830-90 engine was developed in the event there were problems with the more complex two-stage, two-speed supercharger used with other versions of the engine. (NMNA)

F4F-7

Above: The F4F-7 was developed as a long range photo-reconnaissance version of the Wildcat. It had non-folding wings that were wet, meaning that they were essentially large fuel tanks. Total fuel capacity rose to 555 gallons, and this quadrupled the range possible with the standard Wildcat. Cameras were carried in the aft fuselage, but the F4F-7 had no guns or armor protection. To provide the pilot with better visibility, a larger windscreen was fitted which did not have the usual vertical frames or bulletproof glass. An autopilot was installed to reduce pilot fatigue on flights that could last as long as twenty-five hours. Twenty-one F4F-7s, BuNos. 5263 through 5283, were built, and at least two were used at Guadalcanal. An additional one hundred were ordered, but they were completed as the last batch of training F4F-3s during 1943 instead. *(Grumman)*

Right: To dump a large amount of fuel quickly, fuel vents were located in the tail. *(NMNA)*

F4F-7 1/72nd SCALE DRAWING

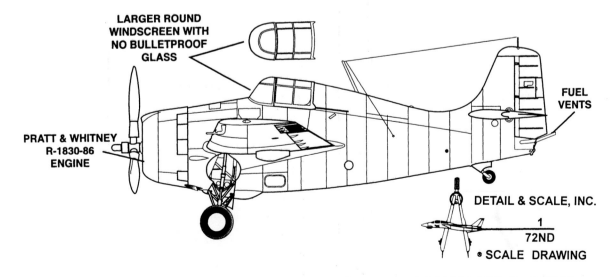

LARGER ROUND WINDSCREEN WITH NO BULLETPROOF GLASS

FUEL VENTS

PRATT & WHITNEY R-1830-86 ENGINE

DETAIL & SCALE, INC.

1
72ND
SCALE DRAWING

DETAIL & SCALE, 1/72nd SCALE COPYRIGHT © DRAWINGS BY LLOYD S. JONES

XF4F-8

The first of two XF4F-8s, BuNo. 12228, was completed with the standard vertical stabilizer and rudder used on previous production versions of the F4F. It also originally had slotted flaps as shown here, but these were later changed to the same split flaps as used on other Wildcats. Note the shorter cowling for the Wright R-1820-56 engine and the exhaust arrangement which is similar to that used on production FM-2s. (Grumman)

In 1942, the Navy issued a request for a lightweight fighter that could operate from the small escort carriers that were joining the Atlantic and Pacific fleets in ever increasing numbers. Grumman's answer was to lighten the Wildcat's airframe and give it a more powerful engine.

The French had ordered the G-36A with the Wright R-1820 engine, and these aircraft later became Martlet Is. Additionally, Martlet IVs also used the R-1820-40B. By the time the Navy requested the lightweight fighter, Wright had further developed this powerplant to the R-1820-56 version, and the -56W and -56WA with water injection followed. It was this uprated version of the engine that Grumman installed in two XF4F-8s, BuNos. 12228 and 12229. It offered 1,350 horsepower, and a Hamilton Standard propeller was fitted to the engine. Each of the engine's nine cylinders had an exhaust stub, so ports were located on each side of the fuselage above the wing as well as under the forward fuselage.

The first XF4F-8 originally had slotted flaps, but these were subsequently replaced with the same split flaps found on other Wildcat variants. This aircraft also had the same vertical tail as previous versions, but flight tests soon proved that this was inadequate to counter the torque of the more powerful engine. This problem was particularly noticeable during takeoffs and when doing a go-around after a waveoff from an approach to a carrier landing. As a result, the second XF4F-8 was completed with the taller vertical tail and rudder that became standard on the FM-2, and the first XF4F-8 was retrofitted with the taller vertical tail as well.

DATA

Version	XF4F-8
Number Built	2
Armament	4 X .50-caliber machine guns
Powerplant	Wright R-1820-56
Horsepower	1,350
Maximum Speed	321 mph at 16,800
Initial Rate of Climb	3,125 feet-per-minute
Ceiling	36,400 feet
Wingspan	38 feet
Length:	28 feet, 11 inches
Height:	
Original	11 feet, 9 inches
As modified with taller tail	12, feet, 9 inches
Empty Weight	5,365 pounds
Gross Weight	7,080 pounds
Maximum Internal Fuel	117 gallons
External Fuel	2 X 58-gallon tanks

Flight tests revealed that a taller vertical stabilizer and rudder were needed to counter the increased torque of the R-1820 engine. Therefore, the second XF4F-8, BuNo. 12229, was completed with this taller vertical tail, and it became standard on production FM-2s built by Eastern. (Grumman)

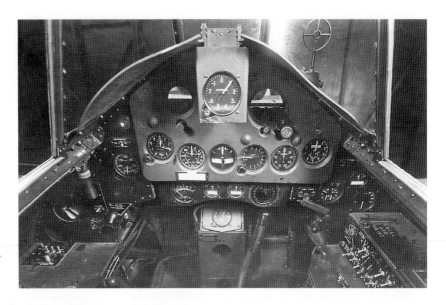

Right: Details on the XF4F-8s' instrument panel included extra gages to measure the aircraft's performance.
(Grumman)

Below left: The items on the left side of the cockpit were like those found in a standard F4F-4. Primary among these were the throttle quadrant with the engine and propeller controls, trim tab controls, supercharger control, flap selector, and the fuel tank selector switch.
(Grumman)

Below right. The electrical distribution box, radio equipment, and landing gear hand crank remained the major features on the right side of the cockpit.
(Grumman)

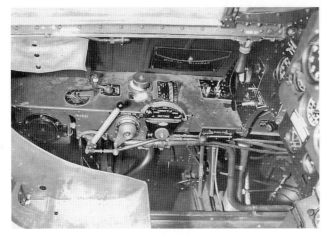

XF4F-8 1/72nd SCALE DRAWING

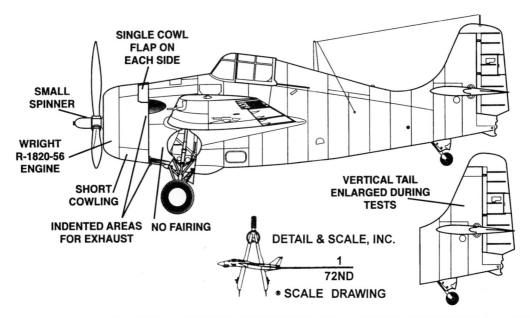

SINGLE COWL FLAP ON EACH SIDE

SMALL SPINNER

WRIGHT R-1820-56 ENGINE

SHORT COWLING

INDENTED AREAS FOR EXHAUST

NO FAIRING

VERTICAL TAIL ENLARGED DURING TESTS

DETAIL & SCALE, INC.

1
72ND
SCALE DRAWING

DETAIL & SCALE, 1/72nd SCALE COPYRIGHT © DRAWINGS BY LLOYD S. JONES

FM-1

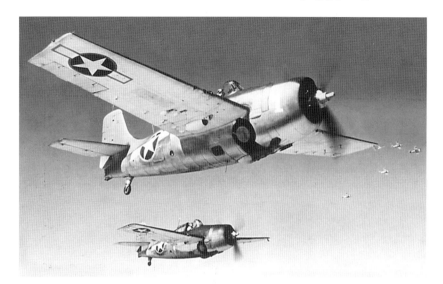

An underside view of an FM-1 in flight illustrates the return to the four-gun arrangement preferred by most pilots. This is evident because there are only two ejector slots for the spent shells and links under each wing. Otherwise, the FM-1 was identical to the F4F-4 built by Grumman. These Wildcats are painted in the tri-color camouflage scheme, and they have the short-lived red surround on the national insignias. *(NMNA)*

As Grumman concluded deliveries of 1,169 F4F-4s, production of the Wildcat was well underway at General Motors' Eastern Aircraft Division at Linden, New Jersey. The final F4F-4 was completed at Grumman in May of 1943, and by this time, the production lines at Eastern had been operating for over nine months. As the move to Eastern occurred, the Navy changed the designation from F4F-4 (Fighter, 4th type, Grumman, 4th version) to FM-1 (Fighter, General Motors, first type). An initial contract for 1,800 FM-1s was issued on April 18, 1942, and the first flight of an FM-1 took place on August 31, 1942. However, only 839 FM-1s were completed before production was discontinued in favor of the more powerful and significant FM-2.

The FM-1 was identical to the F4F-4 except that the machine gun armament was returned to the four-gun arrangement with the increased ammunition load of 1,720 rounds.

Some FM-1s were assigned to the composite squadrons that embarked on escort carriers, while others were assigned to training units as Hellcats and Corsairs began to replace the Wildcat in front line fighter squadrons during 1943. Other FM-1s continued to serve on escort carriers until large numbers of FM-2s became available.

FM-1s took part in the Navy's operations in the Gilbert Islands during November 1943. These included sixteen FM-1s on each of the escort carriers LISCOME BAY, CVE-56, CORAL SEA, CVE-57, and CORREGIDOR, CVE-58. In January 1944, FM-1s participated in the Marshal Island operations and again the escort carriers CORAL SEA and CORREGIDOR were present. Additionally, during this action FM-1s also operated from the escort carriers MANILLA BAY, CVE-61, NASSAU, CVE-16, and NATOMA BAY, CVE-62.

The Royal Navy took delivery of 311 FM-1s which it initially called Martlet Vs, but in January 1944, the British decided to change to the American name for the aircraft, so they became known as Wildcat Vs instead.

This FM-1 was assigned to VC-55 aboard USS BLOCK ISLAND, CVE-21. It is painted in the Dark Gull Gray over white paint scheme that was used in the Atlantic, although the demarcation between the two colors is difficult to distinguish in this photograph. It appears to have the red surround on its national insignias, and this looks to be rather rough on the fuselage. Shortly after this photograph was taken, BLOCK ISLAND was sunk by a German U-boat. A color profile of this aircraft appears on *page 34.* *(NMNA)*

DATA

Version	FM-1
Grumman Model Number	G-36B
Number Built	839
Armament	4 X .50-caliber machine guns
Powerplant	Pratt & Whitney R-1830-86
Horsepower	1,200
Maximum Speed	320 mph at 18,800
Cruising Speed	191 mph
Initial Rate of Climb	2,200 feet-per-minute
Ceiling	34,000 feet
Maximum Range	1,280 miles
Combat Range	838 miles
Wingspan	38 feet
Length	28 feet, 10.5 inches
Height	11 feet, 9 inches
Empty Weight	5,895 pounds
Gross Weight	7,975 pounds
Maximum Take-off Weight	8,762 pounds
Maximum Internal Fuel	144 gallons
External Fuel	2 X 58-gallon tanks

Top: Many FM-1s were used in training units in the United States. This tri-colored Wildcat was assigned to Fighter Training Squadron Ten at NAS Atlantic City, New Jersey. (NMNA)

Right: British style rocket launch rails were evaluated on this FM-1. Four rails were installed under each wing, and they were mounted in a staggered arrangement in pairs, one above the other. These were not used operationally, however late FM-2s were fitted with six zero-length launch stubs for 5-inch rockets. Also note that the approach light remains on the leading edge of the left wing just outboard of the guns. (NMNA)

FM-1 1/72nd SCALE DRAWING

DETAIL & SCALE, INC.

$\frac{1}{72ND}$ SCALE

● FIVE-VIEW DRAWING

FM-1 (MARTLET V)

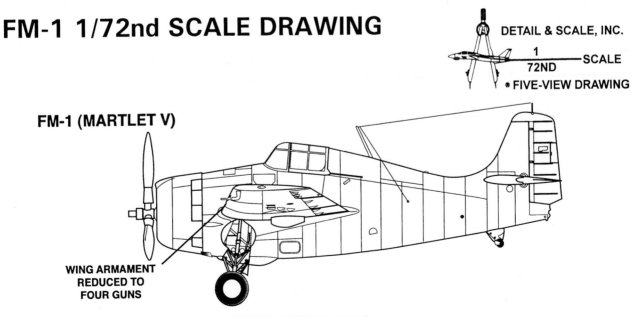

WING ARMAMENT
REDUCED TO
FOUR GUNS

DETAIL & SCALE, 1/72nd SCALE COPYRIGHT © DRAWING BY LLOYD S. JONES

FM-2

FM-2s from the operational training unit at NAS Jacksonville, Florida, fly formation in late 1944. These aircraft are painted in well worn tri-colored camouflage schemes. Note that the antenna mast on the spine of each aircraft is vertical rather than being slanted. FM-2s usually had a bullet shaped propeller hub, but these training aircraft are fitted with the same stepped hub and Curtiss Electric propellers found on previous American versions of the Wildcat.   *(NMNA)*

Grumman developed two XF4F-8s in answer to the Navy's request for a small lightweight fighter that could operate from escort carriers. These two aircraft served as the prototypes for the FM-2, which became the final and most numerous of all Wildcat variants. Deliveries of FM-2s from Eastern began in September 1943, and two Navy squadrons quickly began service evaluation of the new "wilder" Wildcat. During the first half of 1944, FM-2s began to be assigned to composite squadrons aboard escort carriers in the Atlantic and Pacific fleets. In the Atlantic, the escort carriers provided air cover above the convoys all the way from the United States to Great Britain. In the Pacific, the aircraft from the escort carriers spent much of their time flying close support missions for the ground forces, but they also flew anti-submarine patrols and performed various other support roles.

Once in service, the FM-2 quickly proved to be the answer to the Navy's request for a lightweight fighter for its escort carriers. It was over five-hundred pounds

lighter than an F4F-4, and with a more powerful engine, its performance was significantly better at lower altitudes. The engine alone saved 230 pounds of weight when compared to the Pratt & Whitney R-1830-86, but because it only had a single-stage, two-speed supercharger, its performance at higher altitudes was not as good as the F4F-4 or FM-1. This was intentional, since it was primarily intended to perform anti-submarine and close air support missions at lower levels where high altitude performance was not important. Although they also provided air cover above the convoys, any enemy aircraft that might attack the ships would do so at the lower altitudes for which the FM-2 was optimized.

The Wright R-1820-56 powerplant was installed in the FM-2, and most were the -56W or -56WA versions with water injection for wartime emergencies. A tank carried enough water for ten minutes of operation with the water injection system. On the earlier versions of the Wildcat that were powered by Pratt & Whitney engines, all of the exhaust was discharged through two stubs under the forward fuselage. On the FM-2, each of the nine cylinders had its own stub, and the exhaust was expended at four places around the forward fuselage including two areas above the wings. Details of the FM-2's exhaust arrangement are illustrated on page 46.

Another noticeable physical change was the deletion of the oil coolers under the wings. These were replaced by a single unit located in the accessory compartment behind the engine. The openings for the windows in the lower fuselage remained, but a piece of sheet metal was installed in each of them rather than the clear glazing used on earlier Wildcats. Finally, the propeller was changed. Although a Curtiss Electric product was still used, it was a different design which optimized takeoff performance. This change was necessitated by the limited takeoff space aboard the escort carriers, and even with the new propeller, catapult launches were the usual means of getting the aircraft into the air. The bullet shaped propeller hub was also noticeably different than the stepped design used on previous versions of American Wildcats.

Internally, the reserve fuel tank was deleted, leaving only the 117-gallon main tank, but FM-2s also retained

An FM-2 from VC-70 flairs a little too high as it returns to USS SALAMAUA, CVE-96. Note that it still has two rockets under each wing as it returns to the escort carrier. The aircraft is painted overall Sea Blue and has the geometric markings used late in the war. FM-2s were often flown without the disc covers on the main wheels, so the six spokes were exposed.   *(NMNA)*

The catapult bridle falls away from an FM-2 of VC-36 as it launches from USS CORE, CVE-13, on April 12, 1944. The aircraft is painted in the Dark Gull Gray over white scheme used in the Atlantic. Note that this Wildcat has the high pressure pneumatic tire on the tail wheel. This was developed to replace the hard rubber tire used for carrier operations on earlier variants.　　　(NMNA)

An overall Sea Blue FM-2 from VC-79 recovers aboard USS SARGENT BAY, CVE-83, on March 25, 1945. On this FM-2, the aft end of the radio antenna wire is attached to the leading edge of the vertical stabilizer, while on the aircraft in the photo to the left, the wire is attached to the stub mast on top of the rudder like on earlier Wildcat variants.　　　(NMNA)

the capability to carry two external 58-gallon tanks under the wings. Because of the reduced internal fuel capacity, the external tanks were used frequently on FM-2s. Beginning with FM-2, BuNo. 57044, the size of the main tank was enlarged slightly to 126 gallons.

To increase firepower, particularly in the close-support role, zero-length launch stubs to carry six five-inch rockets were added beginning with FM-2 BuNo. 74359. FM-2s retained the four-gun arrangement in the wings, but unlike the FM-1, the muzzle of the inboard gun on each wing did extend forward of the leading edge. However, the amount it extended was not as much as on the F4F-3 or F4F-3A.

Production of FM-2s ended in May 1945 with a total of 4,437 being delivered. This made it the most numerous Wildcat variant by a wide margin. As production ceased, a grand total of 7,905 Wildcats of all versions had been completed. At that time, the F8F Bearcat was being built at Grumman to become the Navy's new lightweight fighter. The first squadrons of Bearcats were on their way to the Pacific when Japan surrendered, so F8Fs never saw action during World War II.

DATA

Version	FM-2
Number Built	4,737
Armament	4 X .50-caliber machine guns
Powerplant :	Wright R-1820–56 or -56W or -56A or -56WA
Horsepower	1,350
Maximum Speed	332 mph at 28,000
Cruising Speed	164 mph
Initial Rate of Climb	3,650 feet-per-minute
Ceiling	34,700 feet
Maximum Range	1,310 miles
Combat Range	900 miles
Wingspan	38 feet
Length	28 feet, 11 inches
Height	12 feet, 9 inches
Empty Weight	5,542 pounds
Gross Weight	7,431 pounds
Maximum Take-off Weight	8,221 pounds
Maximum Internal Fuel	117 gallons
External Fuel	2 X 58-gallon tanks

FM-2 1/72nd SCALE DRAWINGS

DETAIL & SCALE, INC.

$$\frac{1}{72ND}$$ SCALE

• FIVE-VIEW DRAWING

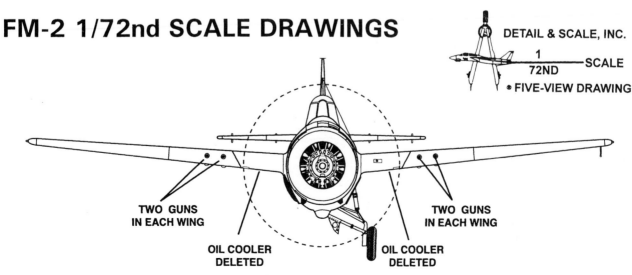

TWO GUNS IN EACH WING

TWO GUNS IN EACH WING

OIL COOLER DELETED

OIL COOLER DELETED

DETAIL & SCALE, 1/72nd SCALE COPYRIGHT © DRAWINGS BY LLOYD S. JONES

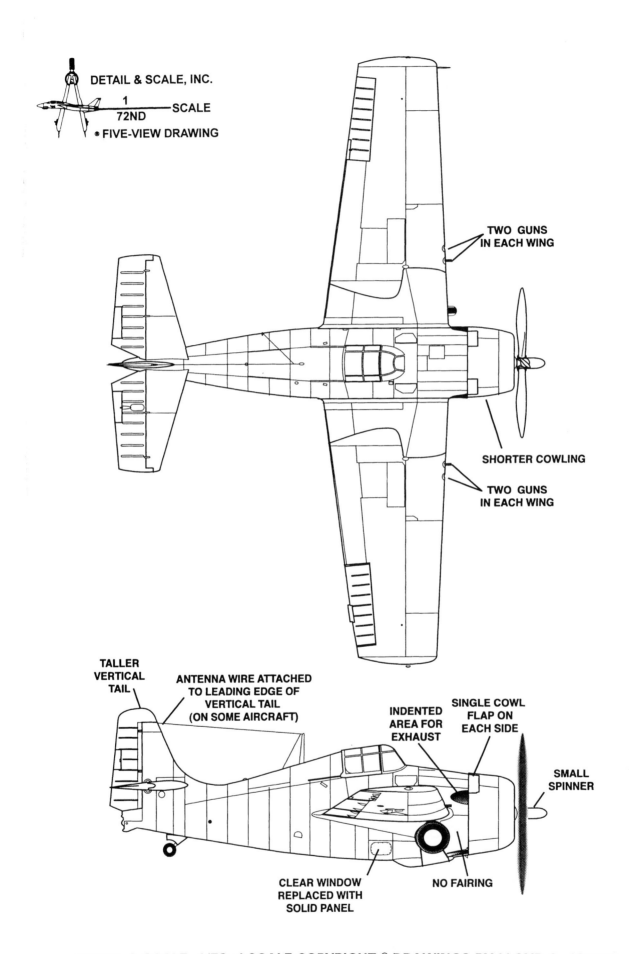

DETAIL & SCALE, INC.

$\dfrac{1}{72ND}$ — SCALE

⊛ FIVE-VIEW DRAWING

TWO GUNS
IN EACH WING

SHORTER COWLING

TWO GUNS
IN EACH WING

TALLER
VERTICAL
TAIL

ANTENNA WIRE ATTACHED
TO LEADING EDGE OF
VERTICAL TAIL
(ON SOME AIRCRAFT)

INDENTED
AREA FOR
EXHAUST

SINGLE COWL
FLAP ON
EACH SIDE

SMALL
SPINNER

CLEAR WINDOW
REPLACED WITH
SOLID PANEL

NO FAIRING

DETAIL & SCALE, 1/72nd SCALE COPYRIGHT © DRAWINGS BY LLOYD S. JONES

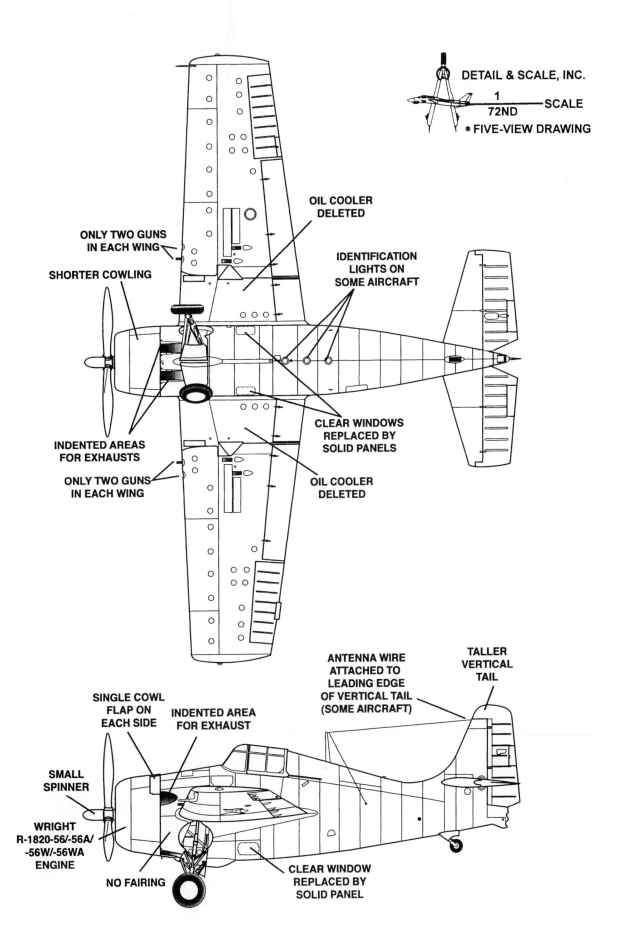

DETAIL & SCALE, INC.

$\frac{1}{72ND}$ —— SCALE

⊕ FIVE-VIEW DRAWING

OIL COOLER
DELETED

IDENTIFICATION
LIGHTS ON
SOME AIRCRAFT

ONLY TWO GUNS
IN EACH WING

SHORTER COWLING

CLEAR WINDOWS
REPLACED BY
SOLID PANELS

INDENTED AREAS
FOR EXHAUSTS

ONLY TWO GUNS
IN EACH WING

OIL COOLER
DELETED

ANTENNA WIRE
ATTACHED TO
LEADING EDGE
OF VERTICAL TAIL
(SOME AIRCRAFT)

TALLER
VERTICAL
TAIL

SINGLE COWL
FLAP ON
EACH SIDE

INDENTED AREA
FOR EXHAUST

SMALL
SPINNER

WRIGHT
R-1820-56/-56A/
-56W/-56WA
ENGINE

NO FAIRING

CLEAR WINDOW
REPLACED BY
SOLID PANEL

DETAIL & SCALE, 1/72nd SCALE COPYRIGHT © DRAWINGS BY LLOYD S. JONES

FRENCH G-36A

The first G-36A produced for the French is displayed shortly after completion at Grumman's plant. The G-36As had the Wright R-1820 engine, and a Hamilton Standard propeller was fitted. Note the short rounded hub that was different from the ones found on American Wildcats with Curtiss Electric propellers. The blades are broader and have much more rounded tips than those on the Curtiss Electric propellers. *(Grumman)*

In the late 1930s, the French had two aircraft carriers, JOFFRE and PAINLEVE, under construction. They chose Grumman's model G-36 to equip the fighter squadrons that would operate from the two ships, and they placed an order in October 1939. Called G-36As, the aircraft in the French order had several notable differences when compared to the Model G-36 being developed for the U. S. Navy as the F4F-3. Most importantly, they were powered by a civil version of the Wright R-1820 which was designated the GR-1820-G205A-2. It was fitted with a Hamilton Standard propeller and provided 1,200 horsepower for takeoff. To test this powerplant on the G-36 design, Grumman installed it in the third and fourth production F4F-3s which it redesignated XF4F-5s. The French also specified that the G-36A would be armed with four Darn 7.5-mm machine guns with two being mounted in the cowling and two in the wings. Oddly enough, the French preferred a throttle that worked backwards from the usual standard. Power was increased by pulling the throttle to the rear and decreased by pushing it forward.

The first G-36A was completed and painted in an overall light gray scheme with French insignias on all four wing positions. The rudder had three vertical stripes, being red, white, and blue, from front to rear, and the French Navy's anchor insignia was painted within the white stripe. The first French G-36A, coded NX-G1, made its first flight on May 11, 1940.

Seven aircraft were nearing completion when France surrendered to Germany, so the Royal Navy took over the order. These seven aircraft were reworked to British standards, and the remaining aircraft in the order were completed to these standards as they came off the assembly lines. In service with the Royal Navy, they became known as Martlet Is.

The G-36As were to have four 7.5-mm Darn machine guns, two of which were to be mounted in the cowling like on the XF4F-2 and XF4F-3. The French markings included three vertical stripes on the rudder which were red, white, and blue from front to rear. (Grumman)

BRITISH MARTLETS & WILDCATS

The Royal Navy took delivery of eighty-one aircraft from the original French order, and these were designated Martlet Is by the British. **(Grumman)**

Like the Americans and the Japanese, the British had recognized the value of the aircraft carrier, and the Royal Navy had several fleet carriers in service and under construction when World War II began. But most of the fighters the British planned to use on its carriers were navalized versions of the Supermarine Spitfire and Hawker Hurricane. These proved to be less than satisfactory, and as a result, the British later ordered large numbers of the American F6F Hellcat and F4U Corsair, because they were specifically designed for carrier operations. These were usually assigned to the Royal Navy's fleet carriers.

Heavy losses in the convoys, Britain's lifeline to America, prompted the development of several methods of carrying aircraft aboard escorting ships. One of these included launching a Hurricane from a catapult for a single mission, after which it would be ditched at sea. Other methods were almost equally inadequate and impractical. The ultimate solution was the development of the escort aircraft carrier. Like the U. S. Navy, the British recognized that Grumman's model G-36 would be ideally

Martlet IIs were powered by the Pratt & Whitney R-1830-53C-4G engine with a single-stage, two speed supercharger. All but the first ten had folding wings, and some that did had the pitot probe moved to the top of the left wing near the aileron as shown here. These Martlet IIs are aboard HMS ILLUSTRIOUS. **(Grumman)**

suited for operations on these small carriers.

When France fell to Germany, Britain took over the order of G-36As that had been placed by the French in October 1939. The French had specified that their aircraft be armed with four Darn 7.5-mm machine guns, two of which were mounted in the cowling. The British changed the armament so that all four guns were located in the wings, but the outboard guns were positioned much further out on the wing than on other four-gun arrangements found in subsequent Wildcat variants.

The Royal Navy named the aircraft from the French order Martlet Is, and the first were delivered on July 27, 1940. They were modified for Fleet Air Arm service by Blackburn Aircraft to include the installation of British radios. But Martlet Is still did not have all of the equipment necessary for carrier operations, so they were used only from land bases. Their first assignment was with Number 804 Squadron at Hatston. On December 25, 1940, two of these Martlet Is scored the first aerial victories by the Wildcat family of fighters when they shot down a Ju 88 that was attacking ships of the British fleet in Scapa Flow in the Orkney Islands. Lt. L. L. N. Carver, RN, and Sub Lt. Parke, RNVR, flying Martlet Is, BJ515 and BJ526, scored the kill which was also the first victory of World War II scored by an American built aircraft. Because of this, the British sent the propeller from BJ526 to the U. S. Navy.

Today, the oldest surviving member of the Wildcat family is Martlet I, AL246, which is on display at Yeovilton, England. It is all that remains of the ninety-one Martlet Is that were completed. Only eighty-one saw service with the Royal Navy, because ten were lost at sea enroute to England.

Martlet IIs were Grumman design G-36B, and they were powered by a Pratt & Whitney R-1830-53C-4G engine that had a single-stage, two-speed supercharger. This was equivalent to the R-1830-90 used in the American F4F-3A, however the British fitted it with a Curtiss Electric propeller with a ten foot diameter. This was slightly larger than the one used on American aircraft. The propeller had a longer hub with a more pointed nose than that found on the Martlet I.

The first ten Martlet IIs had rigid wings, but the remaining aircraft had folding wings. Some of those with the folding wings had the long pitot probe on the leading edge of the left wing replaced with a cranked probe lo-

The Martlet IV was generally similar to the F4F-4 except that it was powered by the Wright 1820-40B engine to which a Hamilton Standard propeller was fitted. This is the first of 220 Martlet IVs delivered to the Royal Navy.
(Grumman)

cated on top of the wing near the aileron. Evidence indicates that Martlet IIs with AM serial numbers had this type of pitot probe, and Martlet IIs with AJ serial numbers had the pitot probe like that used on the F4F-4, FM-1, and FM-2. Later, the first ten Martlet IIs were retrofitted with folding wings.

Martlet IIs became the first variant to be used aboard British carriers when Number 802 Squadron embarked on HMS AUDACITY. This was the first British escort carrier, and it was converted from a captured German merchantman. These Martlet IIs scored the first carrier based kill by a member of the Wildcat family on September 20, 1941, when they shot down a German FW 200C Condor. However, the Germans gained retribution when they sank AUDACITY on December 21 of that year.

The first thirty F4F-3As were originally intended for Greece, and they were already in transit when Greece was evacuated by the Allies. The British took the thirty aircraft and named them Martlet IIIs. Being the same as the American F4F-3As, they did not have folding wings, so the British operated them exclusively from land bases. They were assigned to Number 805 Squadron, and they participated in operations in North Africa.

Martlet IVs, of which 220 were delivered to the Fleet Air Arm, were generally similar to the F4F-4, except that they were powered by a Wright R-1820-40B engine with a single-stage, two-speed supercharger and Hamilton Standard propeller.

A total of 322 Martlet Vs were completed, but only 311 reached operational service with the Royal Navy. They were identical to the U. S. Navy's FM-1. In January 1944, the British decided to use the American name for the aircraft, so Martlet Vs were renamed Wildcat Vs.

FM-2s became the final variant to be delivered to the Royal Navy, and these 340 aircraft were named Wildcat VIs. A patrol of Wildcat VIs scored the Fleet Air Arm's final victories of the war when they shot down four Bf 109s over Norway on March 26, 1945.

Almost 1,100 Martlets/Wildcats saw service with the Royal Navy during World War II. Martlet Is and Martlet IIIs served only from land bases, but the rest operated from aircraft carriers. The British used these carriers and their aircraft almost exclusively in the Atlantic, but a brief trip to the Pacific by HMS FORMIDABLE resulted in the only victory over a Japanese aircraft by a British Martlet or Wildcat when a Mavis flying boat was shot down by Number 888 Squadron.

FM-2s in British service were called Wildcat VIs, and 340 served with the Royal Navy. The landing gear on this Wildcat VI collapsed when the pilot made a hard landing aboard a carrier.
(Grumman)

MARTLET 1/72nd SCALE DRAWINGS

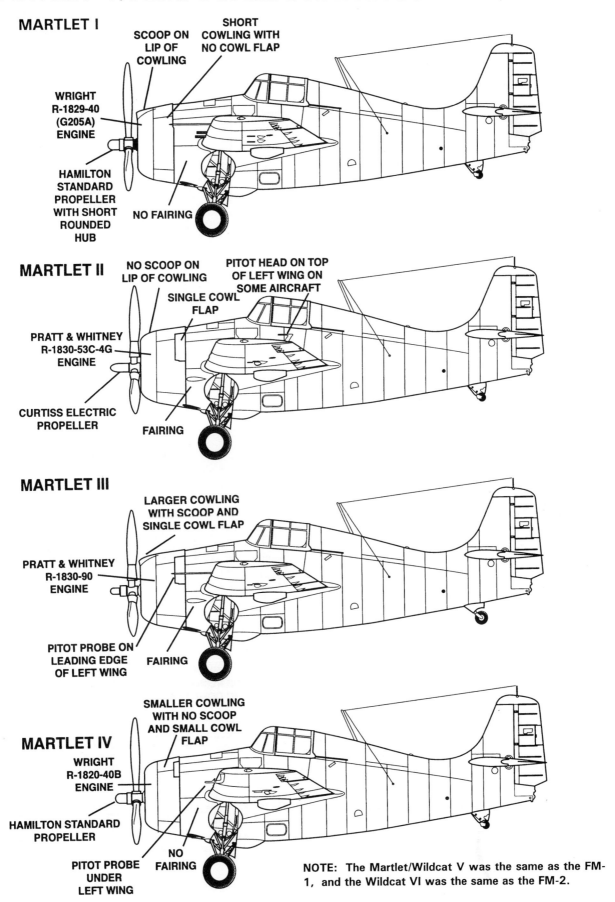

MARTLET I

SCOOP ON LIP OF COWLING

SHORT COWLING WITH NO COWL FLAP

WRIGHT R-1829-40 (G205A) ENGINE

HAMILTON STANDARD PROPELLER WITH SHORT ROUNDED HUB

NO FAIRING

MARTLET II

NO SCOOP ON LIP OF COWLING

PITOT HEAD ON TOP OF LEFT WING ON SOME AIRCRAFT

SINGLE COWL FLAP

PRATT & WHITNEY R-1830-53C-4G ENGINE

CURTISS ELECTRIC PROPELLER

FAIRING

MARTLET III

LARGER COWLING WITH SCOOP AND SINGLE COWL FLAP

PRATT & WHITNEY R-1830-90 ENGINE

PITOT PROBE ON LEADING EDGE OF LEFT WING

FAIRING

MARTLET IV

SMALLER COWLING WITH NO SCOOP AND SMALL COWL FLAP

WRIGHT R-1820-40B ENGINE

HAMILTON STANDARD PROPELLER

PITOT PROBE UNDER LEFT WING

NO FAIRING

NOTE: The Martlet/Wildcat V was the same as the FM-1, and the Wildcat VI was the same as the FM-2.

DETAIL & SCALE, 1/72nd SCALE COPYRIGHT © DRAWINGS BY LLOYD S. JONES

MARTLET I

DETAIL & SCALE, INC.
$\frac{1}{72ND}$ —— SCALE
® FIVE-VIEW DRAWING

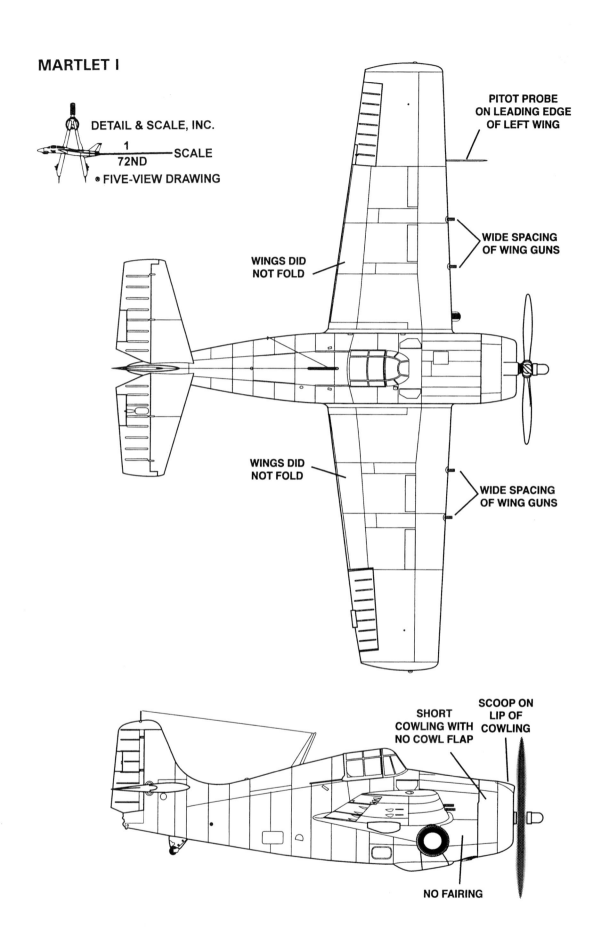

PITOT PROBE
ON LEADING EDGE
OF LEFT WING

WIDE SPACING
OF WING GUNS

WINGS DID
NOT FOLD

WINGS DID
NOT FOLD

WIDE SPACING
OF WING GUNS

SHORT
COWLING WITH
NO COWL FLAP

SCOOP ON
LIP OF
COWLING

NO FAIRING

DETAIL & SCALE, 1/72nd SCALE COPYRIGHT © DRAWINGS BY LLOYD S. JONES

MARTLET I

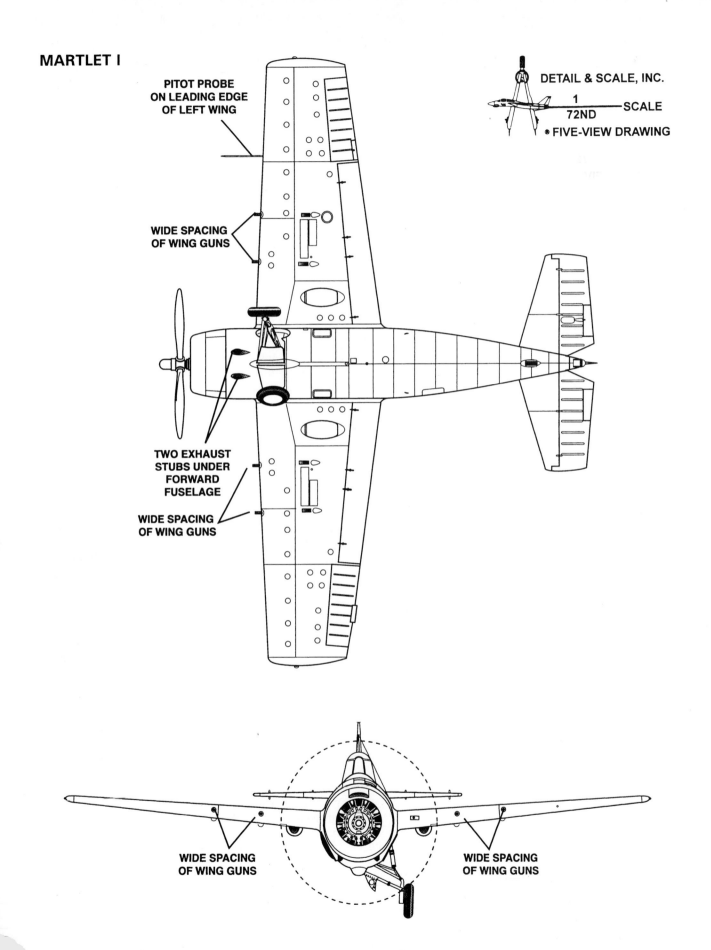

PITOT PROBE
ON LEADING EDGE
OF LEFT WING

WIDE SPACING
OF WING GUNS

DETAIL & SCALE, INC.

$\frac{1}{72ND}$ ——— SCALE

⊛ FIVE-VIEW DRAWING

TWO EXHAUST
STUBS UNDER
FORWARD
FUSELAGE

WIDE SPACING
OF WING GUNS

WIDE SPACING
OF WING GUNS

WIDE SPACING
OF WING GUNS

MODELERS SUMMARY

Note: Each volume in Detail & Scale's "In Detail" Series of publications has a Modelers Summary in the back of the book. The Modelers Summary discusses the injection molded plastic model kits of the aircraft covered by the book, and all common modeling scales from 1/144th through 1/32nd scale will be included. Highlights of the better kits in each scale will be discussed, and recommendations will be made with respect to which kit or kits in each scale are the best for the serious scale modeler to use. Once a kit has been purchased, the modeler should compare the various features of the kit to the drawings and photographs in the book to determine how accurately and extensively they are represented. He can then decide what, if any, correcting or detailing work he wants to do to enhance the appearance of the model.

J. C. Bahr used the Hasegawa 1/72nd scale kit to build this colorful model of an F4F-3 from VF-72. (Liles)

1/144th SCALE KITS

Only one 1/144th scale F4F Wildcat kit has been released and it was by Revell. It represented an F4F-4, but an FM-1 could be represented simply by filling in the outboard shell ejection slots under the wings.

The kit consists of thirteen pieces molded in blue-gray plastic and a clear canopy. A two-piece stand is also provided. The propeller needs to be reshaped and cuffed, and the landing gear is quite basic as might be expected on such a small model. Some thin plastic rod can be used to detail the main gear assembly and add the missing struts and links. The cockpit is open and has no interior, but some thin plastic card can be used to add the basic details including a seat, side consoles, and an instrument panel. An antenna mast and a pitot probe also need to be added from scrap plastic. But the basic shape is accurate, and with a little effort, the finished model will be a nice addition to a 1/144th scale collection.

Hasegawa has also released a Wildcat model in its Mini-Planes series that is actually a re-release of a previous Bachman model. It measures out to be about 1/440th scale, and there is not a noticeable difference from the more standard 1/144th scale. However, this model is plagued with deep panel lines, and the wings are molded to the fuselage with no dihedral. There is a very noticeable dihedral on the real Wildcat. Further, there is a dihedral on the kit's horizontal tail, but there should be none. The parts are generally very heavy and crude.

The only advantage of the Hasegawa kit is that it is presently available, however we strongly recommend using a Revell kit if one can be found.

1/72nd SCALE KITS

Numerous Wildcat/Martlet kits have been released in 1/72nd scale over the years, and most of them are quite dated. Among these are offerings from Airfix, Aoshima, Frog, Hawk, Revell, Minicraft and MPM. The Airfix kit, also released under the MPC label, represented an FM-2, as did the Hawk model. However, the Hawk kit came with the landing gear molded in the retracted position, so the finished model had to be displayed on a stand.

Unfortunately, a good 1/72nd scale model of an FM-2, the most numerous of all Wildcat variants, has never been released. MPM reissued the Minicraft kit with extra plastic parts that included crudely molded fuselage halves that had the taller vertical tail and upper exhaust ports of the FM-2. However, these fuselage halves did not have the slots for the wings or horizontal stabilizers, and they did have an inaccurate representation of the fairing on each side of the fuselage just forward of the landing gear. These fairings were not on the FM-2. Also included among the new plastic parts were a Wright R-1820 engine, lower exhaust ports, the aft end of the fairing for the catapult bridle hook, an arresting hook, and a tail gear with the pneumatic tire. These plastic parts were all molded softly, and some flash was present. Unfortunately, the correct propeller and spinner was not included. Etched metal cockpit detailing parts and a vacu-formed canopy were also provided, but the kit still left much to be desired. We recommend converting a Hasegawa F4F-4 to an FM-2 instead. This will be more time consuming, but it will result in a much better and more accurate model. Of the remaining older 1/72nd scale Wildcat models, those from Minicraft and Revell are the better choices, but they fall far short of the newer Hasegawa kits.

The first 1/72nd scale Hasegawa kit of the Wildcat to be released was an F4F-4, and it very accurately represents that variant. The only real problems are that the cockpit has a full floor rather than having the correct foot troughs beneath the rudder pedals, and the interior of the wheel wells is open. To solve these problems, True Details produced an excellent resin cockpit detailing set that also included the interior for the wheel wells. We strongly recommend using this detailing set with any of the Hasegawa 1/72nd scale Wildcat kits. It is True Details item number TD72455. True Details item number TD72011 is a set of wheels for 1/72nd scale Wildcats, and these also will improve the appearance of the finished model.

Molding of all parts is very delicate and detailed, and the panel lines are recessed. The cowl ring has the intake for carburetor air at the top, but the two intakes for intercooler air are missing. Two 58-gallon fuel tanks are included to go under the wings. The windscreen and canopy come as a single clear part, and we suggest that it be replaced with a vacu-formed canopy from Squadron Products. It is item number SQ9105.

A second release of the kit was supposed to be a

Martlet II, but it did not have the cranked pitot probe that was used on many Martlett IIs that had folding wings. However, a different and correct propeller hub was provided, although the propeller itself was not changed as it should have been. Finally, the cowling had the four cooling flaps scribed on each side, but the Martlett II had only one flap per side.

Hasegawa next released the model as an F4F-3, but the kit came with the same wings as the previous two issues. The instructions told the modeler to fill in the wing fold lines, outboard gun access panel lines, and the outboard shell ejector slot with modeling putty and sand it smooth. Plastic plugs were provided to fill in the holes in the leading edge of the wing for each of the outboard guns, but here again, putty should be used as well. Muzzles for the inboard machine guns were provided, and the long pitot probe was to remain on the leading edge of the left wing. It had also been present on the previous releases, but the modeler had been instructed to remove it. Finally, Hasegawa did not change the cooling flaps on the cowling, leaving the four in place on each side. Only a few of the final F4F-3s had this arrangement. Most had only one flap on each side, and that certainly was the case for the F4F-3 for which markings are provided on the decal sheet. The modeler is therefore left to remove the existing flaps and scribe in the correct single flap arrangement. The instructions do not even point out this needed change. We believe it is completely inexcusable for Hasegawa to pass this kit off as a F4F-3, then expect the modeler to do most of the work of converting it.

Another issue of the Hasegawa kit represents an FM-1, but since the FM-1 was identical to the F4F-4 except for its armament, the only change required is that the outboard gun in each wing must be deleted.

The Hasegawa F4F-4 has also been released under the Dragon label. Dragon included a second set of wings and additional parts so that the wings could be built in the folded position. A segment of a carrier deck and some other detailing parts were also provided.

1/48th SCALE KITS

For years, the only 1/48th scale model of the Wildcat was one from Monogram. This was a hybrid, not accurately representing any one Wildcat variant. With its working features, it was more of a toy than a scale model. Finally, Tamiya issued an excellent 1/48th scale Wildcat that represented the F4F-4 version. It remains the only accurate 1/48th scale Wildcat model available.

The Tamiya 1/48th scale F4F-4 is the best Wildcat model in any scale. Its only real problem is in the cockpit, and here again a full floor has been provided. This ruins the appearance of the entire cockpit, and it is an inaccuracy that cannot be ignored. Aires and KMC both produced detailing sets that will correct this problem. The balance tab is missing from the right aileron, but otherwise this kit is very accurate and well detailed. Surface detailing is recessed, delicate, and accurate. Two 58-gallon tanks are provided to go under the wings.

The canopy is molded separate from the windscreen, and it can be displayed in the open position. Although the clear parts are quite good, modelers wanting a can-

The excellent Tamiya 1/48th scale F4F-4 was used by Stan Parker to build this Wildcat that was flown by LTJG. William Leonard of VF-11 at Guadalcanal. (Parker)

opy with a thinner appearance can use the Squadron Products vacu-formed canopy for this kit.

KMC issued excellent conversion parts for the F4F-3 and FM-2 to be used with the Tamiya kit, but complete kits of these important Wildcat variants are still needed.

1/32nd SCALE KIT

The only 1/32nd scale kit of the Wildcat that has ever been issued is from Revell, and it was first released over thirty years ago in 1969. It is quite good, especially for a kit that old, and we recommend using the Smithsonian Series issue, because it has a corrected propeller.

The model represents an F4F-4, and the wings can be built in either the extended or folded positions. They can even be made to operate, but we recommend against doing this, because it will detract from the accuracy. The cockpit does come with openings on each side that allow the pilot to see down through the windows in the lower fuselage, but it still can be improved and detailed. We suggest using Eduard's etched metal detailing set, number 32 015, which is designed specifically for this kit. This set not only provides details for the cockpit, but items for other areas of the model are also included.

Being an older kit, the panel lines are raised, and there are numerous rivets, but these are delicate and easily removed. The panel lines can be left in place or rescribed as desired.

A decent engine is provided, but some ignition wires and other detailing parts will enhance it. The two scoops for intercooler air need to be reworked, because they are too small and incorrect in shape. The scoop for the carburetor air needs to be opened up. Likewise, the landing gear can be improved with the addition of hydraulic lines and other detailing parts made from scrap plastic. Clear parts are well done and include a windscreen, canopy, and the two lower windows.

While not up to today's standards, this kit is still very good with accurate shapes and outlines. It therefore offers the modeler a chance to exercise his skills in detailing a large aircraft model.

More In Detail Titles from squadron/signal publications....

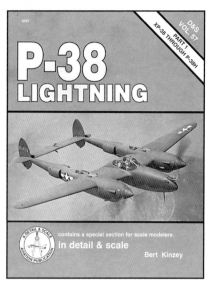

8257 P-38 Lightning Part 1

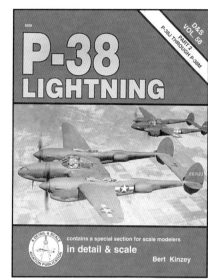

8258 P-38 Lightning Part 2

8260 B-25 Mitchell

8261 P-40 Warhawk Part 1

8262 P-40 Warhawk Part 2

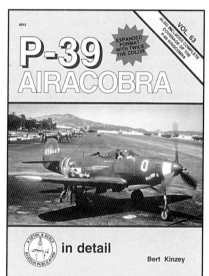

8263 P-39 Airacobra

8264 B-24 Liberator